Among Whistling Thorns

Joan Booth

ISBN: 978-9966-757-4-1-8

Foreword

"What are you up to, Mum?" my daughter asked, finding me deeply engrossed in trying to make my thick fingers tap the right fiddly little keys on my iPad.

"Writing a Foreword for Aunt Joan's book," I replied. Then I quoted the wise old saying: "Oh that the Good Lord the gift could gi'e us; to see ourselves as others see us!"

This book is my aunt Joan Booth's true autobiography as she wrote it in 1978, but it portrays only what she thought of herself; she felt she was no heroine, but a "poor timorous beastie" anxious to "crawl into my funk-hole." As I read it now, I see a woman who cared for others and made a big impact on many – including myself.

Born in June 1900 in England, Joan was the youngest of the six surviving children of John and Ada Booth. Some four to five years younger than Cicely, her nearest sibling, Joan lived, played and dreamed in her own small world, peopled by her vivid imagination.

She paints such poignant pictures of her early life that one can almost see that little plump girl in her button boots and layers of petticoats, fleeing from beneath the giant beech-trees thrashing in the wind. She describes herself as "lacking in spunk," happy by herself, but shy to the point of illness when in a crowd.

Joan did not go to school until she was 12, and then kept missing out through illnesses - strange unexplained fevers. Going to three different boarding schools in search of a healthier climate must have added to her lack of confidence, and being constantly urged to do better and never praised for her achievements did not help.

Nevertheless she lived and loved and laughed with all the wide range of people she encountered across the years in many lands. Her lovely sense of humour bubbled up, even in the most trying circumstances, and her arms embraced all sorrows. She would take on every challenge to help others – often at great cost to herself – and fight those fears of which she was so ashamed. She never said, "No," to all the children who came under her wing, even when it broke her heart to send them back to their own home and family when their need for her was ended.

I know, for I am one of them. I will always love her.

- Celia Owles, Naivasha, November 2017

CHAPTER 1

Early Years

Bank Parade is little known, even to people living in Preston. It is tucked away at the end of a long Lowry-like street. Suddenly the little houses stop; the land drops steeply to a wood and a great curve of the river Ribble. Beyond, across the fields are many railway embankments, factory chimneys, black and rose red, and then the lovely line of Rivington Pike and the western bastions of the Pennines. To the immediate right, on a shelf, is the Parade. Early Victorian and decorous, it keeps the grace of the previous century. The road, being private, is extremely bumpy, and used to end in splendid gates, which opened into two parks, each with its sooty laurels, flower beds set out like carpets, band-stand and fountain. There were two rather frightening railway arches, a continual noise of shunting and puffing with the clink-clink BANG of goods trains, while the expresses would slow down with dignity as they entered the station.

Somehow, though out of sight, this station dominated the place; and certainly it was very grand in the age of steam. There were fourteen platforms for the London North Western and the Lancashire and Yorkshire Line, which boasted it was the busiest goods line in Britain, as well as taking literally millions of folk down to the Lancashire coast during the Wakes weeks.

The station had, still has, I hope, vast waiting rooms and restaurants, built when the railway pioneers thought big. Huge and lofty, with tons of plate glass and mahogany, they were ready to deal with the hordes, which rushed in for food and comfort before lavatories and dining cars came into use.

Indeed, Queen Victoria herself would break her journeys for a meal until, legend has it, a homely old soul stuck her head round the door crying in patriotic fervour, "Ee, Sithee, Yon's Queen!"

It was at this pleasant, railway-haunted place, I was born, the youngest of six children. Half country, half town; a place which seemed almost a family preserve, so many aunts and uncles lived there, as well as the italianate villa at the end, which had housed my grandparents. A sunny place, with gardens running down to the river, where I sat in my lovely perambulator made from elaborately woven cane under a rug embroidered with two very green Egyptian cats sitting side by side, staring at me with black eyes, solemn and satisfying, while I smelt the spicy Gloire de Dijon roses growing up the house.

The backs of the houses looked into horrid dank yards. The back wall, as high as the bedroom windows and edged with straggly privet, was the haunt of love-lorn, belligerent cats. It is a wonder the children of Bank Parade survived suffocation, as I think we all spent the night under the bedclothes with our fingers in our ears to block out the ghastly row, which had a ground bass of gurgling, wheezing plumbing.

Number ten had something extremely exciting, which gave us children a sense of superiority. From the front cellar, which was the laundry, there ran an underground passage. Beneath the pavement and road it emerged from under a rustic arch of limestone and periwinkles onto a drying green. With terrible clarity I remember standing on the garden steps leading to the gate screaming with terror as I saw a large pack of brown dogs pouring out of it into the garden. Whether it was an hallucination, or whether there were two or three dogs to give me this fright, I still do not know. All I know is that I yelled and my brother put his arm round me to comfort me. Of course I never spoke of it until now, so I am still left wondering. The house was double fronted. To the left the dining room was a perfect period piece with green wallpaper, turkey carpet and red leather seated chairs, which matched the overmantel and sideboard in light oak. This last had a delightful recess, just the right size for a bunk, if you happened to be a sailor at the time. There was a sofa and Father's chair, which had knobs that could be twisted, making the back go down in a magical way. In the window was a polar bear skin, its stuffed head fitted with glaring eyes and gnashing teeth, which Father had brought back from the North Cape along with other treasures. There used to be a photograph of the group of intrepid tourists there, some sporting tam-o'-shanters or deerstalkers. Father, very disappointingly, was only wearing a bowler hat. On the mantelshelf stood two large cloisonné vases and a black marble clock, shaped like a Grecian temple, known as "The Mark of Esteem" because a silver shield on its base said so. It had been given to Father and Mother by the firm as a wedding present. The mark of esteem frequently fell off. This had no sinister meaning for my parents were much loved and esteemed. Then, of course, there were the pictures. Both Grandfathers collected dozens. It was the custom after a meal for guests to be shown these pictures in most houses at that time, even when you did not have a long gallery full of ancestors. Our pictures, we thought, were nicer than other people's, and I still think they were, especially the tranquil one of ships by a Dutch painter, and the Sidney Cooper of cows and a pollard willow with a lovely sunny view across fenland to a church tower.

One of my early memories is of standing by the breakfast table clasping a huge grey elephant. He had a kindly face and I loved him, and announced that his name was Tim. I could not understand the embarrassed gentle laughter of the grown-ups. It was Uncle Tim who had given it to me, so this was very daring on my part, verging on cheek. But Tim he was until, many years later, moths destroyed him.

The drawing room, across the hall, is a vague memory. Grandpapa Kenyon sitting in the bow window (he had a very large bow window himself and a splendid chestnut beard) took my slate and wrote on it.

I can see the curly numbers now, though at three years old they meant no more than Chinese characters, so I must have disappointed him. Another time there was a tea party. Very elegant it was, and after the meal I sat on Mother's blue-grey silken lap, whilst one of the guests, famous for her fine voice, sang. She began pleasantly enough but then rose to perfectly unbearable screeches. It was so awful that I slid to the floor and bolted. Listening in the hall I waited until the song became quite gentle again, so I cautiously ventured in, but shot out when it

Joan Booth's maternal grandfather, John Kenyon.

rose to those unattainable high notes. It was extremely rude of me and I had a good scolding, but Mother owned that she would have liked to have done the same.

This room held a magical piece of furniture – an elaborate lacquered cabinet brought by my other Grandfather from Japan. Every sliding panel, little drawer or cupboard had landscapes on them, little boats cruised amongst wooded islands where there were thatched houses and far away mountains, or there were designs of swirling water in which fishes swam. Here were treasures - Roman tear bottles, ivory chopsticks, emus' eggs and, best of all, a square of amber with a fly embedded in it, even older for it might have sat on Adam's nose! At the top was a niche in which stood a black lacquered box whose two little doors opened to show a golden interior and the Buddha seated on his lotus throne. Some people were quite shocked that an idol should be given place of honour in a Christian house, but I am grateful that my parents felt otherwise and gave this bright tranquil thing its right setting.

Now-a-days houses do not seem to have room for special treasures, which is a great deprivation. To be allowed to hold - very carefully - something rare and strange is a great treat. Even if it is only something

4

out of Grannie's workbox, or a tin of old buttons, it is more than entertainment, or for keeping you quiet. It gives a sense of values, history and respect.

Behind the dining room was the nursery-cum-morning room where the Hepplewhite chairs were - bought because they were beautiful, although very old-fashioned. There was a small black upright piano and two rocking chairs, splendid things for playing circuses or racing across the room, though you might get a nasty toss. A dark room but richly golden with its yellow wallpaper and plushy upholstery. I had my breakfast there and like all children, played islands with my porridge, though there came a day when there was a row because I refused it when someone sploshed black treacle on, saying I must eat it up because my Grandpapa liked it. I still find this to be wholly illogical and worthy of a strike.

Children are truly honest people and should be treated as such. Cicely had been furious, and quite rightly, when taken to meet a cat whose doting owner said could talk. The animal responded to her blandishments with the usual cat noises and never a rational word of greeting, so Cicely felt cheated. Then there was trouble when she and I were urged to sing a dotty verse, which went, "Good night Papa, Good night Mama, Good night to all the rest," ending, "But I love dolly best!" This was wholly untrue as we had little use for dolls; also the parents were Father and Mother. It was a footling tune as well.

Next door was a small pantry where one was allowed to dry the spoons, and then a long darkish kitchen with its black and steel range, where the Sunday joint hung in a big tin thing with a clockwork contraption on top which made it revolve before the blazing fire. There was a grey parrot in one corner, and splendid smells of bread and parkin (gingerbread cake). Cook tried to teach me to make a cross-stitch kettle holder, but I didn't get the hang of it, and there was one truly dreadful day when she tried to cheer me up. Why I needed cheering up, I do not remember. She galumphed up and down singing, "See me dance the polka." It was awful; like a camel in pink cotton frock and apron - all ungainly angles and enormous feet. I rolled about with my fingers in my ears. Poor Emma.

In the spring of 1906 came a great day when we moved into the country. Long afterwards my mother told me how her heart had sunk when they went to view Barton Hall. Standing a quarter of a mile from the high road and some four and a half miles north of Preston, it was a large rambling building, modernised in 1770 by the owners, the Shuttleworths of Gawthorpe, who had obtained the estate by marrying the Barton heiress in the early 17th century. It had been sold to a Mr Jacson in 1810. When my parents saw it, the estate had been split up, while the house had stood empty for twelve years, apart from the east wing, occupied by a gamekeeper-farmer. Ceilings had fallen in, water had to be pumped by hand, the roof leaked and, of course, it had no form of lighting. Apart from the occupied bit, the house had huge rooms, three staircases and halls and any amount of long passages. It stood in a large garden with acres of shrubberies on a sandy hillock overlooking a park which had been skilfully planted with variegated trees at a time when an educated gentleman knew about making the most of contours and vistas. What made it irresistible was the mile and a half of excellent trout fishing. Father could rent it at a ridiculously small sum if he made repairs, and as he drove away he patted Mother's knee saying, "I know you will make a lovely home of it," which she did.

John Booth,
the author's father.

Ada Booth, nee Kenyon,
the author's mother.

We were not well off, but water and electric light were laid on and the local joiner and builder fought the dry rot. Being the seventh son, he had, by local custom, been christened Major, and he had a terrible stutter, so bad you really wondered if he was going to have a fit. But he was a marvel when it came to using his hands. The spring water which fed the hand-pumps was crystal clear and cold; our new supply came from the fells and, though very soft was, in fine weather, the colour of strong tea. In wet, the colour and consistency of cocoa. You had to hang on to the soap and guests had to be persuaded to bathe in it. We never did manage to get the roof watertight, often having to rise up in the night to place buckets at various spots.

Aunts rallied to help with the furnishings. The long Georgian windows with their shutters which, when I was tall enough, were my job to close at night, were curtained, with art serge costing, I think, a shilling a yard, and edged with strips of Indian embroidery in wool on tough material costing even less. Indian rugs could be had from about ten shillings apiece, and looked well on the polished floors. We all acquired good sea legs. Unfortunately, the visitors were apt to skid. Wallpaper went up in the bedrooms after ten layers were stripped off, and the other rooms painted pleasant colours. It was about this time that Grandpapa Kenyon died, so added to our own stuff were plenty of massive pieces, including a very long walnut grand piano, a Broadwood with a delicate high pitch, and a full-sized billiard table. It took up part of our main sitting room, leaving plenty of space for sofas and chairs round the fire, an elegant sideboard and a piano. Also quantities of oil paintings and steel engravings with more watercolours for the drawing room.

Mercifully there was a most ancient furnace in the huge cellars and large iron pipes took the heating to stacks in all three halls, elaborate things which, very stupidly I think, were topped by grey marble slabs. The last squire's wife wrote her memoirs and stated with no shame that she had had the carved wooden chimney pieces removed, installing in their place vast marble ones, fortunately not as horrible as they might have been. There were still the Georgian ones in the back rooms.

Of the actual move I cannot remember a thing. What is indelible,

7

Joan Booth in 1904, at four years of age.

coming to me in my dreams, are the inexhaustible mysteries of the buildings, passages and stairs in both house and farm. A hundred years before, the squire had kept hounds, so there was a ramification of kennels, now the abode of hens, and many horseboxes, stables, coach houses, shippons and barns, the cheerful harness room, brew-house and laundry, all with cobwebby rooms above, and two very small cells, now used for provender, but useful in the old days when Squire was a J.P. Best of all for play was the cobbled courtyard with its pump and tunnel-like entrance, where the great double doors, with the little one set in one of them, had innumerable bolts and locks; splendid they were for playing castles and prisons.

The farm was run by handsome Mr Thornton, who had a fierce dog and ferrets. His gentle, careworn wife made the butter up into lozenge shaped pats stamped by a wooden mould, to be taken with eggs and garden stuff, to market on Saturday. There was a delicate daughter Lizzie and two young sons. I looked with awe at the two elder ones when they came visiting, one being a policeman and the other a signalman on the railway who, having lost a hand, used an iron hook with great skill. "Our Billy" looked after the ponies and drove the dogcart; "Our Dick" spent most of his time on a sofa, out of doors in the summer, as he had a mysterious illness known as hip joint disease.

I tried not to be frightened of the cows but preferred them tied up when I could swing on the half door watching the milking, even being allowed to try on a good-natured beast. Later there was a poor white cow, which reared and kicked whenever Cicely went past. This was because she had read a story in the *Boys' Own Paper* in which a man had had to out-stare a bear in the Rocky Mountains. There being no bears handy, she sat on a railing and fixed her large brown eyes on those of a calf. Both were motionless for some twenty minutes. Cicely had no ill effects from this staring match, but the calf never got over it, as far as she was concerned, being quite normal with other people. My delight was the hens, a splendid mixed bunch. Speckled, Plymouth Rocks, Buff Orpingtons, plump Wyandots and those neurotic Leghorns, which seem to have taken their place, all sorts of crossbreeds and the colourful bossy cocks. They ranged about at will, laying wherever they chose. Every morning bran and 'seconds' were mixed in a bucket with boiling water. It was delicious. "Fancy Joan eating hen food after an ample breakfast," they cried, not knowing that years later wheat germ and bran would be sold for health food at high prices.

This reminds me that an important cleric came to preach at our Church, and asked us to have pity on the very poor, especially the mothers of big families who had difficulty in making ends meet. Afterwards our farming friends couldn't understand why a woman should find it difficult to make hen food. Whereby we digress into the matter of dialect, which is mostly old English, just as our Cumberland maid years later used cates for eatables - I had thought she said 'cakes', at which she snorted and made it clear that the wedding feast was furnished with all sorts of delicious food.

Beyond the kennels and barns, under a very ancient oak, was a six-sided little building with a thatched roof. Mr Thornton would bring the day's bag of game here, moving those hung on hooks in the beams up higher and putting the day's kill on the lowest hooks. It was not until I was grown up that saying a bird was 'high' connected up to the actual fact that it had come from a hook high in the larder roof.

All this complexity had a maze of cart tracks and drives each having a gate with its own squeak and clang where you could swing, gazing out over the valley and brook, to rising woods waist deep in swimming bluebells. Most of them forbidden ground because of the pheasants, though once over the white footbridge you went up through one on an age-old path leading to the high road, and the station lane where two trains a day kept us in touch with town. This lane had lost its old name of Boggarts, and I still want to know where the Boggart lived and who it was. Another lane had a pond haunted by a man and a horse. Mr Thornton scoffed at this, having passed it often at night and seen nowt. Years before, the farmhouse close by had its thatch removed and a saddle and sword turned up amongst the straw. People remembered that the man who farmed there had become prosperous after one of the Jacobite risings and conjectured that a paymaster slipping north by this lane had been ambushed and disposed of.

It was a place full of delights, wonders and terrors. To watch carpenters fashioning things. The skill needed in keeping the banks of the brook in order, a whole-time job, when stakes were driven in and the gaps filled with brushwood. This seems a forgotten art now so that the water sweeps away banks and plasters good grazing land with cobblestones and sand. The terrors were pig killing day, when a very alarming man drove up to deal with the poor things, and those when gales blew, making the huge beech trees groan and creak. Then I would play in the courtyard, until bidden to go out into the nice fresh air. The only place safe from these giants was the acre of walled garden, a great way off for a small fat girl scuttling in panic under the thrashing boughs.

Once there, all was peace and order. Box-edged beds, gravel paths and a blue pump at the centre. Red currants were trained up the north wall between the morello cherries and pears and plums on the other walls, which had flues to warm them from the spring frosts. There were rows and rows of gooseberries and a very long tunnel of rusty iron rods under which you could walk and look up at the brilliant emerald and scarlet of even more red currants. To the south outside were decayed glass houses, a big tank where there were the newts, which the country folk called asps and said were deadly poisonous. Then the ladies' garden, which was a knot garden of interlacing beds, full of old roses and good smelling plants. The whole place, along with the shrubbery edged with box, needing trimming each year, along with beech and yew hedges as well. Mr Croft and Abraham, the lad, managed the lot with no hurry. Both had splendid voices and would sing the 'Te Deum' as they hoed. Mr Croft came from Pilling on the coast where we got the peat used in the house. He had married one of our cooks and lived in the square little lodge. Very snug they were, I thought, as I sat on his knee by the bright fire singing 'Whilst Shepherds watched their flocks by night' together, or listening to 'The Cuckoo is a pretty bird.' He was full of country lore, just as Mr Thornton was, who made a point of telling the bees any family news. He cured Cicely's earache by taking cut willow twigs, putting one end in the fire, catching the sap as it oozed from the other end in a teaspoon, and putting it down her ear. He said she would never have earache again and nor did she. He did not know that the Latin name for willow is Silex and that the acid in the sap is connected with aspirin and can be used for dissolving wax. Mr Thornton's remedy for colds was jolly and practical, "Yo mun, drink rum and honey. Not in t'pub but in bed, and yo mun stay there till your shirt's dry."

The wild garden, sloping towards the second little brook, was really a warren. The whole garden would have been one but for buried slates, wire fences and constant vigilance. You left a door or gate open for a moment and the chase was on. At morn and eve rabbits came loping onto the lawns, nibbling peacefully right up to the windows, even into the house during the first year we were there. Also there was the constant cry of 'The cows are in!' (One cow knew how to unlatch the iron gate). Then they must be shooed out very gently lest the great heavy things began to slide, removing rolls of turf off the lawns.

These were mown by Polly, fat brown with a hogged mane. She wore leather boots for the job. Otherwise, she pulled a small dogcart, and was clever enough to put on a pathetic limp until you got out and looked at her shoes, after which she gave up the game, but had her revenge by shying all over the road if she saw a fluttering bit of paper. I found this alarming but Mother quelled her at once. She also knew how to open the door of the provender store. Her very large round quarters couldn't get through, but the important end found the maize bin.

Our other pony was Maisie, bigger and prettier, just the same bright chestnut as the best dogcart. She would take us into town for shopping. The parcels went under the seat, which was then adjusted to take the extra weight.

There must have been a homestead on this hill, with its good spring water and protecting streams, from very early times. When the old hall was burnt down in 1606, the Shuttleworths moved to what was then known as Barton Lodge, and, as I have written, it was sold in 1810 to the Jacsons (you got your letters back if you put the 'k' in, even though they were in cotton). They squired it there for eighty years. Mrs Jacson was a Fornby of Fornby, and never got over it, as well as being the niece of Sir Robert Peel. Not being strong and living where there were few county families (and then there was the cotton), she retired to her bedroom and reigned from it with the mystery and power of a veiled prophet. Years after she left for her seaside cottage, people spoke of her with awe, especially those who, as children, had been sent once a week from the school that she founded, bearing a note giving the exact moment of their departure. They were questioned as to their progress and it was very alarming as Mrs Jacson had a cane, which came down on anyone whose eyes strayed round the room, or who fidgeted. Even grown men, if they transgressed, were had up on the mat and, it was said, left broken in spirit. Some said the house was haunted and lights were seen moving from window to window at night, but that was explained when she left. The butler and Mr Thornton stood at the foot of the stairs discussing how to get the Missus down when, without uttering a word, she swept past them and down the long corridor to the porch where the carriage waited for her.

After she died, well in her nineties, some of the furniture came back to the house. The Victorian dining room suite vanished, and a noble mahogany sideboard and circular looking-glass joined the once neglected 18th century chairs and dining table, so that the room matched its period,

I am setting all this down, not because it still means so much to me, but during the Second World War it was taken over by the RAF, becoming a very hush hush place, where radar was used and perfected. The courtyard where cart horses would bring the peat and coal became the Ops' room; another story was added and huts went up all over farm and paddocks. Gun emplacements encircled it and the old magic went.

It does not seem to have been a merry house in the Jacson's days. Our smaller household was very different. Besides the tuneful gardeners, the three maids kept the place shining and sang as they worked. Sunday evenings were spent round the Broadwood piano skipping from hymn to hymn. The upright piano in the billiard room had a pianola in its midriff. If we weren't peddling through Beethoven or the gloriously rowdy Washington Post March, we were singing away from fat volumes of songs bidding somebody to drink to us only with their eyes or roaring Polly Wolly Doodle. We were brought up on legends of the Halle. Great-grandfather had been a member of the Manchester Musical Society, which I imagine was its forefather. He was a jolly man who, after a good dinner, would cry "Let's praise the Lord," grab his 'cello, tune up and with his family burst into some joyful bit of Oratorio. Grandfather had a most enormous bass and utterly un-self-consciously would step out of his seat and, standing by the conductor, join in the Hallelujah Chorus with tremendous verve.

In Preston there were at least three music halls where we girls did not go and the Theatre Royal, all cream and gold baroque. Behind the red velvet curtains the scene was painted with a splendid picture of a very plump Circassian slave in blue tights, who pranced before an eastern potentate, and there was the tremendously exciting sound of the orchestra tuning up. I dimly remember pantomimes with a fat girl dressed in a boy's brown velvet suit singing about 'pansy faces' and at the end some lovely lacy scenery. Far better and dear to this day were I Pagliacci and Cavalero Rusticana, Not that I understood what they

13

were about, but I won quite a name for myself singing the drinking song while waving a goblet. This stopped when asked to do my turn at a tea-party, and I was stricken with the first fit of shyness in my life, so that I simply could not do my splendid swashbuckling act. Much later on we had a Repertory company that came for a few weeks and ran successfully for well over two years, filling the big Hippodrome, once the leading music hall. Also, between the wars, an Irish Opera Company visited. The music was good and there was the added entertainment of watching for the regular appearance of an hour-glass waisted ginger-haired lady, well on in years, who took the junior tenor parts. She minced about in tights looking like a weather-beaten principal boy, but obviously loving every minute of it. In Tannhauser, Knights solemnly harping away on stringless cardboard harps were only beaten by poor old Tan himself, staggering back from Rome, to die very lengthily and fall puffing to the stage, and the flowering staff, which proved All was Forgiven, placed reverently on his chest, whence it bounced up and down until the curtain descended and he could get up to take his bow.

When I was about six or so, I went with my father to Blackpool. He took me to call on an old friend of his. A true Romany, she lived in a dell in the sand hills where the amusement park stands, and her name was Mrs Sarah. She was a weather-beaten, hearty old lady and I sat beside him as they chatted about the old days when he used to visit her as a little boy. Of course, Father was extremely old, probably in his fifties, making Mrs Sarah a she-Methuselah. I envied her snug camp, and was delighted to read lately that what may be her descendants still exist in Blackpool, driving those landeaus, which go clop-clopping down the sea front.

With Mother we often visited a tiny thin old lady who kept rooms for a couple of gentlemen. Mrs Carter had been a monthly nurse working for our doctor. She brought most of us into the world and, on several occasions, saved our lives, and mother's too. She came from that very remote part of the country lying between the rivers Wyre and Lune, where life seems to go on unchanged except for the sound of a tractor. How she began to take up nursing I do not know, but it must have been obvious that she had the Gift. When she was a young lass of seventeen, she was looking after an extremely strong-minded old woman who fairly commanded her to marry her son. Our Albert was a weak character who needed a firm hand. Strangely enough she did so and bore him a son. I never heard anything of him, so conclude he was a nonentity as well as a trial. She told Mother how one night he was drinking away his earnings at the pub, while she kept watch at home. She became so restless that she paced up and down the bedroom with a blanket about her shoulders, longing and longing for him to come home. Suddenly he blundered in at the door, white-faced and trembling. "Yo mun never do that again, Agnes," he cried. On being asked what she had done, he said, "Coomin to me in t'pub, wrapped oop in a blanket an' makin' me tcoom whoam."

She was also gifted with second sight, which distressed her quite a bit. Only once she came to Mother to say that she would be leaving next Wednesday, and on being asked why, said that the doctor would want her to go to a lady in Clitheroe. Sure enough, the letter came, and afterwards Agnes said it was the same woman she had seen that night. "Just the head and shoulders with a shawl round them, but it was the lady who needed me."

CHAPTER 2

Interesting Relatives from my Childhood

At home Cicely and I did lessons while Connie went to school in Scotland and the boys to Yorkshire. There was the long trudge to Church on Sunday, where we had Matins and the Litany. The choir was made up of red-faced farmers and their buxom wives, who cheerfully bellowed to the Lord to have mercy on them as miserable sinners. A less miserable lot you could not find, which was puzzling until Cicely explained the difference between feeling miserable and admitting you were a poor specimen. It was pretty boring when your head didn't come above the pew top and the hassocks hurt your knees, however the church had been rebuilt in pink sandstone, so one bit of entertainment could be had by choosing a stripey square which, if it were ham, would cut up nicely for a large family. On the first Sunday of the month we were let off the Litany and had the Ten Commandments. After the last hymn the whisper, "Are you staying?" went down the pew and I was taken out by the governess, perfectly sure that I should be struck dead had I stayed on. This was so terrible that years later when visiting home I had to be removed from the Anglo-Catholic Church in a state of near hysteria.

This feeling, reduced to a kind of glum dread, lasted on into my thirties, not helped at all by horrid solemn books we were given in our teens - books which urged you to prepare for Communion on Monday with such earnestness that you were convinced that you could never work yourself up to the required intense holiness expected of you. Now when I see small children trotting up to be blessed, looking happy and confident, I thank God, hoping the old way of going about what should be a joy and wonder, has died out.

After Church there was the dusty walk down the high road, then through a wicket gate down the fields and woods to the stream. Just by the footbridge was a spring spilling into a square pool. It never failed; its ice-cold water, lovely to drink and bathe one's face in, has been swept away now.

That stream was the best of playgrounds. There were sandy beaches and cobblestones of every colour. Steep cliffs, very exciting to traverse, and secret places where king-cups and forget-me-nots grew. Thornton showed me the tracks of an otter once, and many a time I crept silently behind Father, watching whilst he dropped his March Brown at the head of a pool, strike with a flick of the wrist and then play his trout until he brought it in for me to scoop into the net. Little ones went back, but some evenings there was a good catch or just one for Mother's breakfast.

Numerous relations came to stay, as well Connie's Scottish school friends. There were two very elegant cousins who wore marvellous dresses of foamy cream lace and long gold streamers. They had taken part in some function when royalty had come to Manchester and showed me how to make a sweeping curtsey. Younger cousins came, with whom I played Cowboys and Indians, and cooked vegetables in an old pan over a fire in the wild garden, to their mothers' horror.

It is not so long ago that a young man referred to "one of my madder aunts," which pleased me greatly. For one thing, I am very much an aunt, and great-aunt, myself, and when I think about it, we looked on our aunts as a quaint lot, and immensely old. Father's sisters dressed well and were chilly, one really terrifying, one an invalid and very beautiful.

Mother's sisters had the Kenyon gusto. Chief of them was Aunt Bea, who after several engagements married a completely cube-shaped

The Aunts on Fathers side were well-dressed and frigid.

Father's sisters were well dressed and frigid.

parson whose Christian name was Heber. His parish lay in the centre of a huge featureless industrial district north of Manchester. So smokey was the air that curtains had to be washed every fortnight. The vicarage garden, besides a few dark grey hens, that should have been white, might produce one or two sunflowers if it was a good summer, although one never really felt the sun's warmth. She gushed in a deep treacly voice, which made us squirm, but let it be remembered that she told my mother that to be a parson's wife in Radcliffe was the happiest life possible. The reason for this extraordinary statement was the size of her heart. She loved every man, woman and child who came her way, weeping with them in their sorrows and enlisting them in what was the only festivity that poor district seemed able to afford. A Hot Pot Supper somehow took on the glamour of Ascot and the Lord Mayor's Banquet combined. She got plenty of entertainment herself from her people.

There was the wedding where the strapping bride bashed her large bouquet across the groom's stomach and shouted, "Speak out," when his "I will," was uttered. Also, she was rather shamefaced but found it funny when at the end of the World War there had been a memorial service. Thinking that many of the bereaved would be overcome, she gathered a bunch of young men, stationing them at the back of the church with orders to lead those who looked as if they might keel over into the fresh air. "And, you know, I think they began to look on it as a kind of sport. They'd say, 'Ee sithee she's swaying, she's got 'er 'ead down, Coom on,' and the poor woman was sitting on a gravestone before she knew who had grabbed her."

She and Heber were very fond of food and were continually asking for just a little refreshment for the other spouse, who was exhausted. The two of them, advancing arm in arm down the streets, filled the entire pavement, never ceasing from waving and calling out to their dear friends. She had a very good way with Bishops. No roast chicken and *Onward Christian Soldiers*, from which they are said to suffer, but a delectable meal and then the sofa drawn up to a bright fire in the drawing room, where it was suggested his Lordship would like to meditate, "and I would peep in ten minutes later to find him fast asleep," she would say, beaming at us.

There was a day when Heber and an almost-as-portly uncle, went for a stroll up the Little Orme in Wales. A fresh breeze was blowing and Bea stood at the bottom and in her melodious voice called: "Heber, Heber dear, do come down, you will be blown out to sea."

They were the star turns of the family. When they died, the shops shut for their funerals and their dear folk lined the streets.

Edith, the next sister, was rather dim and most kind. She preserved a Cranfordian decorum: "I will bid you goodnight," with a graceful bow as she left the room. Poor dear, she was terrified of cows and the least speck of red must be tucked away before crossing the fields. With fiendish glee we would watch her take out her handkerchief, put it to her mouth and, breaking into a gentle trot, cry, "Expectorate, my dears, expectorate," if we came across a really pungent country smell.

Then there was Louise, who died young. Brilliant, gay and gifted, she opened doors of appreciation: "Look how cleverly he has got the flicker of firelight," she said, as we turned over a magazine together, and I can see the picture still.

Mentioning magazines, what a period it was for them! Boys walked along the station platform with a basket strung around their necks bearing a dozen or more, *Windsors, Strands, Wide Worlds*, at sixpence a time! They could be bound for a very few shillings, so that on rainy days you could read about the Maneaters of Tsavo and Calamity Jane (who looked very like cook and not the least like a film star), and there were the whole range of *Punches* from the beginning. Also, big volumes of the *Illustrated News*, best looked at lying on the floor. There were pictures by Caton Woodville of battles where no one was hurt more than clutching an arm or wearing a handkerchief round a brow. Best of all was the *Strand* with the Nesbit stories and the *Captain* with some school stories by PG Wodehouse. For a short while an uncle parked his books with us and there were some - could they have been **The Yellow Book**, I wonder? - full of Aubrey Beardsley and his followers. The swirling designs and gaunt tragic faces haunted me for years with a horrible fascination.

Besides our clerical uncle, there were many more; some of them only legendary figures. One we saw much of was Wilfred, only a little older than my eldest brother. Being a sickly child, grandmama sent him to the famous strong man Sandow, he of the leopard skin, fancy sandals and enormous moustache. Sad to say, Wilfred never wore a leopard skin, though he became a man of tremendous muscle power, able to bend horse-shoes, lift grand pianos and, by way of a joke, use a crowbar bent to look like a walking-stick, which he would gaily toss to some unsuspecting chap. With his gilt hair and quick blue eyes and buoyant spirits, he was all Celt. Grandpapa and Grandmama were first cousins, and of all the big family he was most Kenyon, a family which I am sure proves that there are small pockets of real Britons tucked away in the Pennines.

This uncle took up motoring in the 'nineties. I cannot remember the make of the first car he brought to Barton, only that the passengers got in by a door in the back, as you did in a wagonette. The Aunts pinned brown paper to their moire silk petticoats in order to keep themselves warm and wore the regulation tan leather motoring coats and flat tweed hats lashed on with yards of coloured ninon, which was gathered into a ring and then came round over the ears and round the neck, ending with a splendid bow. Driving was very exciting. We were expected to leap out if there was a stiffish hill and scotch the rear wheels with stones should the brake or engine fail. There was a tremendous lot of brass to keep polished and the lamps gave a dazzling white light and a horrible smell when the acetyline was changed.

My brother, Wyn, soon had a cream-and-red two-seater. I think it was a Darracq; you could hear it coming a mile away. I am told it still exists and am not surprised.

protected from the cold
by sheets of brown paper.

The Aunts pinned brown paper to their silk petticoats
to keep themselves warm while motoring.

People talk about the noise of traffic now. True, you have to be very far in the country for quiet, but I am not so sure that the towns were not noisier in those days. Main streets, apart from the wonderful wooden blocks in the west end of London, were paved with granite setts, but back streets were cobbled, as were the country lanes. As only the grander traps and carriages had rubber-tyred wheels, there was the most tremendous noise. In Preston teams of cart horses drew lorries loaded with cotton bales from the docks and station, up the main street to the mills, and there were delightful two-wheeled floats loaded with salt and scrubbing stones to be traded for rags and old iron. The driver stood upright amidships with the float see-sawing beneath him.

More desirable were the ice-cream carts, canopied and cream-coloured, richly painted with roses and twirly lettering, their ponies having bells on their harness. It was not just the roses and bells which entranced one. It was the way the ice-cream man placed a wafer on a little oblong container, scraped up the cream, plastered it on and placed another wafer on top, delicately turned it out and presented it to the customer. Oh lucky ice-cream man! Oh lucky customer! (We were not allowed the stuff).

Then there were the trams swopping, screeching and clanging as they swept down the streets, stopping to let passengers down just when the rest of the traffic wanted to pass them. As more vehicles came on the road this became such a nuisance that they were done away with. At the height of their time there was a network of them connecting the industrial towns of Lancashire and Yorkshire, and we knew of a clergyman who had such passion for them that he worked out a journey from Sheffield to Liverpool, joyfully treating his family to it. From then on, they loathed them.

On market day hundreds of farmers and their womenfolk drove their traps to town, where the wife would set out beautifully prepared poultry, cheese and butter on a snowy cloth, with often posies of mixed flowers. Only the other day somebody said that with the soaring price of petrol we should revert to traps, or even donkey carts, but what town nowadays can provide stabling for all those beasts, let alone hay and oats and the farmers' ordinary, that huge meal costing a shilling or so, which the dozens of inns provided, and which now no longer exists.

Our first car was an open red Humber bought in 1910. Billy Thornton learnt to drive and was our chauffeur until 1914. Our first long expedition was to Scotland, spending the first night at Windermere. On the stretch between Penrith and Carlisle we had to go very slowly as the road had been mended by throwing loose cobble stones on it and no steamroller had as yet broken them down. When Billy went to the war, Dick took his place. He had improved in health enough to limp about and Father thought an outdoor life would suit him. In spite of little schooling there seemed to be nothing he could not tackle - joinery, electric troubles, house repairs - he would come to put things right as well as being a good gardener. He had a very plain face with a kindly look, and slow, countryman's speech and endless patience.

He married Maggie, a beautiful temperamental housemaid, who nagged him and their one daughter, though Maggie was sentimental over their dog and cat and all of us. For the rest of my parents' lives they cared for us, Maggie coming to the rescue if we were short-handed, for she was a superb cook. She treated me as if I was seven years old until I was a middle-aged woman, having been sent when a maid to see if I was clean and tidy for meals. Years later there was no greater joy for the nephews and nieces than to 'go to Dick's' to eat delectable teas and learn various ways of playing dominoes. I think Dick is one of the saints, especially when I remember that for most of the time he was in pain.

Our best uncle was Father's brother, Fred. He was a doctor, having left the family business young. He crammed at Hawkshead Grammar School, whose headmaster was noted for being a brilliant teacher. He spoke of those years as being paradisal, with the fells and lakes to explore, and squirrels to catch and roast over a fire. From there he went to Aberdeen, where lads still came from the Highlands and Islea with a sack of oatmeal to live off through the term. When we knew him he was married and practising in St Anne's-on-the-Sea, still only a small place, though growing fast. He battled to have wind-breaks and gardens along the front and so prevent it becoming an asphalt jungle, like its great neighbour, Blackpool. He had a long humorous face and could conjure lovely music from the piano. Father and he would be at their happiest going fishing together.

"I'b god a Bad Code" I told him once.

"You haven't, you have a cold," said he and I at once saw that this was so. 'Bad Cold' was an anxious female bit of fuss. I met the same honest precision when Father took me on one of his trips to Liverpool warehouses. In one of these were samples of chestnuts, four or five set out on squares of paper, one of each sample cut in half. "Look," I said, "there's a bad one."

"Well," said Father, "it's an honest sample."

These trips were long and tiring and I am sorry I did not listen more carefully and learn something of the art and mystery of Grocery. I remember rumbling voices discussing tapioca, sultanas, which if bleached were swept aside, currants stoneless and small - large ones were popular in the South.

Back at home, when not scrambling by the brook, there was painting. Lancashire being a wet place, there were days and days given up to it. It was so distressing trying to improve a picture in a book, to find the Prussian blue, always an aggressive colour, had got into the Crimson Lake, so that the princess had a dingy purple face.

Then there were lessons, of course; dear Lora couldn't teach for toffee, as we discovered when we went to school. One of a parson's huge brood from east Lancashire, she had been taught millinery before taking up teaching. Her hats were a kind of engineering job, like building an oil rig, and almost as massive. First wire, then buckram, then the covering, which was often velvet, and the trimming of satin bows - they were monumental. It was the period when hats were wider than a woman's shoulders, sometimes lovely straws with ruched lace on the underside, piled in front with silky pink peonies.

Connie had a very sporting affair in blue suede with nearly a whole pheasant across the top - its tail got a vicious tug from an old body in a tram. Old ladies in their sixties wore black bonnets above those black fitter-length cloaks known as dolmans, hideous with fur and black beads. Mourning being under strict rules – so many months for sisters, cousins and aunts, etc. – that the elderly had hardly time to get out of it, when they were back in again. One of the few good side-effects of the World War was that the holocaust was such that people came to their senses on the matter.

Our clothes were mostly made by somebody in the village, or by a friend who came to stay for a month or so to work away in a back bedroom. She was one of a large family of daughters living at St Anne's, cycling, dancing and playing golf until their father came home. She plonked a five-pound note on the table and said, "That's all the money I have in the world." This in an age when only a strong sense of vocation would make a girl take up a career. So they were doomed to be governesses or seamstresses. Yet, somehow they managed, and our Miss Lithgoe scraped enough together to be able to spend her last years in her own little house.

Of course we wore quantities of underclothes with a complexity of tapes, ribbons and buttons. Those of white linen were sewn on, the bar of thread carefully buttonhole-stitched over to make a dear little caterpillar. Over my combinations were soft quilted stays, to which my knickers were fastened, then a flannel petticoat, the edges scalloped and embroidered, then an overall petticoat, and my frock with a pinafore on top. Knickers, petticoats and pinny were a mass of *broderie anglaise*. Grown-up dresses were made on a lining fitting close to the body, over which would go a jap silk lining and then the drapery of the dress, so there was a great deal of doing up with layers of hooks and eyes or minute buttons set close together. No wonder people in old photographs look more upholstered than clothed, and there was a constant call to come and 'do me up.'

When I left school I was considered old enough for real corsets - not wasp-waisted ones, thank goodness - but laced at the back and fastened by a couple of steel bars which clipped together, keeping you perfectly vertical. "You must expect a little discomfort to have a good figure," the elders said. As yet the 'bra' had not arrived, so a tightly fitted bodice kept one firm in front. It was not at all the thing to call them camisoles. 'Bust bodice' was their name, and much later a very

More upholstered than dressed.

Ladies looked more upholstered than clothed.

young member of the family, seeing this written on a laundry list, remarked that surely 'torn bodice' would be in better taste.

Broderie anglaise edged everything possible, even children's summer hats and coats. Womenfolk were always busy with needlework, in fact it was rather awful if you weren't; and you felt guilty if found reading in the morning. When Mother was young, ladies took their silver or gilt sewing sets out to tea-parties and worked rolls of lawn with the ubiquitous *broderie.* That had died out, but there was still crochet for every tea cloth, mat and pillowcase, or, if pious, for the church. They even sat on the sand at the seaside, crocheting away like mad. No wonder many took up sketching.

We young were almost in uniforms. For best, plain jap silk dresses gathered into a yoke, with a pink or blue silk sash for parties, along with silk socks, and later bronze silk stockings, so thick they squeaked when you pressed them in your hand. Also, lovely supple bronze dancing sandals with fluffy pom-poms. Otherwise it was sailor suits. Blue kilts and striped blouses in summer, scratchy genuine naval serge in winter; both had bibs and collars, difficult to put on as they had so many tapes and loops. Black silk scarf and, with luck, a lanyard. Over these went reefer jackets and a cap with the name of a dreadnought on the front. In summer a large straw sailor hat. Or on Sunday a straw with a white ribbon. I yearned for a wreath of daisies, which a very few lucky children owned.

All these hats were held with elastic bands under the chin. Inevitably, you played with them, when they retaliated by snapping to, giving a nasty sting - and serve you right if you got it during the sermon and couldn't say, "Ow."

About the only change from those sailor suits was to have a smock of unbleached linen, which smelt horrid when new, but was thick with traditional designs. Traditional, too, were the sunbonnets women wore when hay-making or selling shrimps in the market. In winter, for very best, we wore velvet coats with smoked pearl buttons and a tippet and muff of ermine. Nearly all woman carried muffs, and when Mother was a little girl the inexpensive fur for children was chinchilla.

We wore strong boys' boots, though in summer I went barefoot in the garden. In winter there were those leather gaiters with innumerable buttons to wrestle with, while the grown-ups, in a hurry, cried, "Come on," or worse still, tried to push your fingers into tight-fitting gloves, after which you were told to sit still and not touch anything. Mother could remember being sat like that in the hall, all ready for church, whilst nurse cut the scorched ends of her big grown-up brother's trousers. He was just back from Australia when the clipper's cargo caught fire, and they had only made port by keeping the air out of the hold. Day and night they had watched the decks for the least trace of smoke so that the crevice could be pasted over with paper or anything that came to hand. This must have been in the 1860s.

Here let me mention that, in England, in this century, little girls and housemaids did not 'bob' to their elders and betters. I see a lot of it on television and can only imagine that it is put in for the sake of other countries where it is expected. Also in the North, I did not hear servants say 'Madam' until after the First World War, when only some rather toffee-nosed people went in for it. It was 'Mam' or 'Mum.' Of course we were convinced that the South country folk were a stuck-up and, at the same time, inferior lot. There were no real damsons south of Cheshire, and the poor things didn't know how to make horseradish sauce, or Yorkshire pudding, and were practically imbeciles when it came to hot-pot. We were passionately provincial. I still am.

Was not the King, Duke of Lancaster and toasted as such? The best of Shakespeare was John of Gaunt's bit, and all I knew of Milton was that he wrote that "Darwen's stream" was "with the blood of Scots imbued." Up in the trough of Bowland (pronounced Bolland, if you please) was a tiny stream where you could jump into Yorkshire and leap back out of foreign territory, forgetting that our great-great-grand-father on Father's side came from that county. Lancashire is a County Palatine and, though I did not know what it meant, was very splendid. Lord Derby was almost royal, being our tribal chief. There was nothing servile in this, in fact I begin to think that class war is a new idea used to cause division. In the Lake District there is no feeling about it whether a man is an earl, a small hill farmer or a shipping magnate. The last probably, as an off-comer, will have to bide on his land for several generations before being admitted into the close fraternity. At Barton one or two men would touch their forelock, but they looked you in the eye, and in the towns the mill owners' family and the parson's were 'Eur Bill' and 'Eur Bess.'

There was a snobbish gulf between Trade and Mill and County, though it did not show up with people who were genuine or 'jannock,' and later I met people who were touchy about what public school they had gone to.

My brother and many cousins went to Giggleswick, near Settle. The two older ones left early to work at an accountants' office, before starting at the bottom of the family business. Father was at its head known as Mr John because Grandpapa had been Mr Booth. He never seemed flurried, being one of those people who step into a train two minutes before it starts moving. How he managed to take a very real interest in the Blind Home and be chairman for the Blind Societies in the North, and the Orphanage and Deaf and Dumb School, the Electric Company and his own firm, as well as innumerable small kindnesses is a mystery. I think it lay in the peace of heart, which comes from a most simple and loving faith.

In those days our Preston shop was long and narrow. There were chairs along the counter and customers were offered sweets set out in pretty Japanese bowls. Tea and other dry goods were weighed in those brass scales the Figure of Justice holds, and parcelled up in thick purple paper, fastened with string which was broken round the finger in a very enviable way, the whole operation done in a matter of seconds. At the side of the shop a low archway led through into Glovers Court and so to the back door where the horse-drawn vans were loaded. Inside there was a kind of glass box where a very ancient man wearing a velvet skullcap, called a William Tattersall, sat, and had sat from time immemorial, doing the books. There was a tiny office with high desks. It was very dingy and the only decoration was two pictures of Chinese mandarins crumbling in their frames, pictures which had come along with the four-foot-high vases and huge bowls, in the famous tea clippers. Father's office, a bit bigger, had a window and fireplace, a desk and an easy chair, generally occupied by a Roman or Anglican cleric partaking of a glass of sherry. Father's generosity to all denominations shocked some people, God help them.

Under the window ran a long counter where samples were studied, the most important being tea tasting. This last was a solemn ritual. As the new crops arrived, they would come in small round tins labelled with the name of the tea garden and the ship which had brought the tea to England. They were set out in order and an amount weighed in a tiny pair of scales, against a threepenny bit. Each sample went into a white porcelain mug, which had perforations near the top and a neat lid. Water was boiled in what must have been one of the first electric kettles and the mugs half filled, a small hour glass turned over giving them exactly three minutes to brew. In the same order the mugs were tipped so that the tea was strained into porcelain handleless cups, all these standing on a special battered old tray perforated for draining. Time being up, the mugs were put back, long shallow silver spoons came out and the tea was tasted by sucking it very noisily into the mouth, rinsing it round and then spitting it out into a three-foot-high spittoon. Such grave thought was given, accompanied by a ritual tapping of the cups with the spoon and remarks as, "a little sharp, not quite up to last year's." The leaves were inspected and smelt, the discarded cups pushed back and the right blend arrived to make up the teas for which we were famed. The tiny broken tea leaves were sold as the 'siftings,' an idea father pioneered.

One wall of the office was lined with ancient and curiously shaped wine bottles. I am grateful that this respect and knowledge of good things was part of our heritage. It sounds wildly extravagant that we had champagne with our midday Sunday dinner, which was a special treat because it was the only midday meal the menfolk attended. The unspoken rule was that we did not drink wine until we were eighteen and spirits much later as "they were bad for the complexion." Then we were asked our opinion. "Yes, this was pleasanter than last week's; it was cheaper coming from a little known house." Wine was not a treat or more sadly a slightly wicked fascination. You treated it with respect. Also, I cannot remember any of the strange jargon used in describing wine nowadays.

In 1909 when Wyn, the eldest son, was 21, there was a garden party for the firm. Father announced the profit-sharing scheme. He liked the idea of partners rather than employees and had been in touch with Lever's, who had pioneered the idea. It was a glorious June day and the people from our five shops arrived in horse-drawn charabancs (an early kind of bus) and were feasted in the big dining room and hall. The great attraction that year was a gramophone with a very large brass horn, and we stood round marvelling, to hear Caruso and Melba sing *Let me gaze* from Faust and Harry Lauder singing, "I lo'e a lassie." Then the news of the scheme was announced. I can still see an old warehouseman with his cap tilted over one eye as he scratched his head whilst gazing at the strip of paper stating the amount of his bonus, and hear his, "By Goom."

Fervent socialists will say this was frightful paternalism. Surely if we own that God is our Father, good fatherhood is to be recommended?

The parties went on each year until we left Barton. As the staff multiplied, they had to overflow into a marquee on the lawn, and a firm of caterers was brought in to cope, though decorating the tables was my job. During the summer we would have a whole string of parties. The orphans came one day. Given an essay on "What I want to do at Barton," one wrote, "Get myself lost," which would indeed be heaven if you lived in an institution. The Blind Home children would charge across the lawn to the revolving summer house, its axle becoming hot as it whizzed round to cries of, "Anyone for Blackpool?" The first time they came we made the mistake of asking them to raise their hand if they wanted more to eat. Every hand went up and went on going up until all we had left was some bread and butter. When they rose to sing grace, we saw that their tight blue jerseys bulged with great mounds of cake stowed away for future enjoyment.

In the next village was a large house left in the eighteenth century to be a Home for Decayed Gentlefolk. These elderly ladies and gentlemen came too, and once one of them took a nasty turn, collapsing into a chair. "Shall I get some brandy?" Mother asked, to be told that he was a fervent teetotaller, so she got him a glass of creme de menthe. "Peppermint Cordial," she said truthfully and he downed it at one gulp. Speechless and gasping he held out the glass for another swig. Mother never knew whether she had prolonged his life or shortened it, as he died a fortnight later, but he went home in a very jovial mood.

The men of the family worked long hours. Shops stayed open very late at the end of the week, later at Christmas, when they would not get home until the small hours. A fortnight's holiday was the usual thing, so the long summer evenings and half days were very precious. Father would get his rod and go down to the brook. As he said, it was not so much the fish as stepping quietly along the bank that gave him such joy.

Sometimes Maisie would take us in the dog-cart to the little river Brock or up to Barns Fold Reservoir. The trap would be put up at a farm where I could watch big cheeses being made. Here there was a perfect farm kitchen with sanded floor, rag rugs and a rocking chair for the master, snowy tables and brass. Under a long window full of geraniums, we would feast off boiled eggs, home-made bread and currant pasty. At Barns Fold there was a stuffy parlour with a harmonium on which I strummed, trying all the stops. It was just as well the walls were three feet thick. It was here that an orphan lamb tethered to a damson tree, cavorted round me until I was tied up fast and had to yell for help; but most of the afternoons were spent day-dreaming amongst the quaking grass and dog daisies, listening to the lap of water and the call of the curlews.

One evening, going home with Uncle Fred sharing the front of the trap and myself on that very narrow back seat, we passed a motor car, a red one, the panels painted to look like wickerwork, belonging to the maker of Wood Milne rubber heels in Leyland, (you knew all the local cars then). Just as we passed, the car backfired. Father called to me to hang on, and hang on I did, whilst Maisie galloped flat out for a mile or more. She it was who, when Uncle Heber hauled himself into the dog-cart, trotted smartly round to the stableyard, instead of down the drive, to church.

Mother did not come on these fishing trips. Six surviving children out of nine had left her with little strength, though she was always gentle and merry. She was very lovely and must have been a stunner in her youth with her cream skin, blue eyes and massed chestnut hair. Although often laid up, or overcome with attacks of exhaustion, she would soon pick up, going her way spreading friendship and gaiety. The only times I can think of her speaking sharply to me was when she detected a note of whining self-pity in my voice. She would wake early, read her Bible, perhaps write letters or just think about the day ahead, and people. Later she might say that some particular action or plan was right, and it invariably was, being part of the wisdom of God, whom she loved and trusted.

Those were the days when families would play games in the evening. Charades were the best of all, but there were lots of guessing games, and even in hotels she could get a lounge full of bottled-up British having tremendous fun together. The only drawback was that she was telepathic so that the guessing was too easy for her.

32

After her death it was truly comforting to have letters from all manner of people saying how they loved her and how some word of hers had a lasting effect on their lives.

She was careful in having the brightest and prettiest kitchen - the one at the Vicarage had brown paint, five doors and frosted glass windows – and was careful in choosing her staff, seeing to it that Cook was the kind of woman who made a happy home for the other two or three girls. During the war, the maids were in short supply, so we took an orphan. William came from a Catholic Home in Liverpool and looked nine-tenths Japanese. He had been sent to the farm, gone down with pneumonia and needed easier work, so he cleaned the boots and knives. Soon he was waiting at table in a pepper-and-salt uniform with large shiny buttons. Our little Scots cook resented it if Mother had cause to tick him off, though the 'poir wee bairn' was as bright as his own buttons. The only time he lost his head was when we were having a big party. He had been ushering guests in like a full-blown butler until a large family arrived, and he shot into the drawing-room crying, "Mrs Booth, they're coomin' in doozens!"

Those were the days when each bedroom had its marble-topped wash-stand with the elaborate set of china, jug, bowl, soap and sponge dish, toothbrush holder, carafe and glass, and double sets for the double rooms, along with a slop bucket and chamberpots. Hot water came twice daily, and you were trained to knot the sleeves of your nightdress round your waist and give yourself a thorough good wash in the mornings with a flannel, which really was a piece of flannel. One of the economies of the house was the use of plain bar soap, the basis of fancy scented soaps, though I suspect the spare room had a tablet of Margerison's Buttermilk. Of course, we pined for the scented kind, and I still feel it to be an exotic luxury. There was a water-closet off the courtyard. The one upstairs was at the far end of a very long passage, and it was years before we had one indoors downstairs, to everyone's relief. Of course it was the housemaid's job to do the slops armed with buckets, disinfectant and cloths, and the mind boggles at what they had to cope with before water-closets and bathrooms were installed, and families were enormous.

See me dance the Polka!

Cook in a good mood, dancing the polka.

Having connection with the Electric Light Company, we had what was a very early vacuum cleaner, a big clumsy thing it was too, and the maids seemed to prefer the good old-fashioned way of sprinkling the carpets with tea leaves and sweeping by hand. More popular was the electric iron, which did away with the flatirons heated on the kitchen range. On baking day dough was set to rise on a steel stool by the fire. Sometimes Cook would give one a bit, which turned curiously grey when kneaded, so it was better if she made a dear little mouse with currant eyes. When baking was done we would beg for the kissing crust - the bit that curls over the tin. Broken off, whilst warm, well buttered and sprinkled with demerara sugar, it is superb - the real sugar butty - I have known children of quite civilized families who have never tasted one - poor things!

Of course, there was the great wooden clothes rack lowered away by ropes from the ceiling where things were aired, often acquiring a strong smell of roast beef. It also dried out the big flabby oatcakes until they were brittle.

We did not get an outside telephone until the 1920s; we had a house phone from the billiard room and the parents' bedroom to the kitchen, to save long journeys. It really was a boon to be connected with the outside world and was a friendly thing, so that you could chat to the operator, who once, when I asked for a number said, "You'll not get him, he's downt'garden feeding t'dooks."

During these years I went in for 'Joan's feverish attacks' and very nasty they were, with horrible rumbling nightmares. Sometimes old Doctor Brown would come out in his horse-drawn carriage, leave a bottle of medicine, and entertain me by whistling down his keys on a big bunch so that he could play tunes. More often Mother would resort to a cold compress, a cure which must have gone back to ancient times.

Stripped naked, my fiery body was wrapped in a sheet wrung out in cold water - (how I yelled!) - and a blanket rolled round me like a cocoon. After the first shock it sent me to sleep, to wake up with temperature down. That meant sitting up in bed, a white shawl pinned round me and old volumes of *Punch* to look at. In spring a Jaffa orange to eat with a spoon, like a boiled egg, was a special treat.

One hot summer's day in 1909 Connie was out on the lawn when her urgent calls made Mother look out of an upstairs window to see Monsieur Bleriot in his aeroplane flying up from the south and over the house. He had just crossed the Channel and the *Daily Mail* had sponsored his attempt to fly from London to Edinburgh. It seems, in hindsight, that he was flying so low we could see him sitting up there amongst the struts and wires. This put my brothers into a passion to fly too. Strong calico was bought and much bamboo, but Father or someone talked them out of it.

Next it was the Coronation year with a field day with sports and

Awful behavior at a tea party.

mugs for the children, coconut shies and a very small roundabout worked by hand by a very large beery man.

By this time Connie was grown up, wearing vast hats and hobble skirts so tight at the hem she couldn't get into cars or over stiles. There was also a gigantic fuss over the 'harem skirt.' That was a very long dress with the hem caught between the ankles. It surely should have been taken as a sign of extreme modesty, but curiously people thought it was the opposite. I saw one brave woman wearing this garment in Fishergate and heard the onlookers in an upstairs cafe, saying how shameless and dreadful it was.

We also had in Preston a brave lady, the wife of a doctor, who was that frightful thing, a Suffragette. She dressed her little son in strange arty tunics, delightfully comfortable, but they made us giggle. The mildest views on women's rights branded people as belonging to those awful women, who put lit matches into letter boxes and burnt Lord Leverhulme's country house on Rivington Pyke. They were out to make a nuisance of themselves and did, yelling their slogan in theatres and concert halls. It took courage to go to prison, even to drive a governess cart swathed in suffragettes' colours down Fishergate to the boos of the crowd. The violence created a stalemate of stubbornness, so the non-violent could not make their views known, and it was a mercy that the work done by women in World War I earned them the vote, even if the other half of the reason for the concession was the fear the whole wretched business might start up again.

Wyn had joined the Terriers in 1908, which was when they were founded. Taking the Mayor to church twice a year wearing a scarlet jacket, sword and a very policeman-like helmet, he would also go into camp for a fortnight in summer. He escaped catching enteric, for some men died of it due to the army bringing back the wooden water-carts, which had been used in the Boer War. His bedroom was a shrine of masculinity, with his sword, guns and photographic groups of himself and his fellow-officers, whom I worshipped. There was an Irish adjutant to whom I lost my heart completely. At that age a small girl's heart is wide open. The pew behind us was filled with a farmer's family and one son, I worshipped simply because he was called Ambrose, a name which bowled me over. Then there was a middle-aged Quaker friend who ran a paper mill at the top of a lonely valley in the fells. He was a pioneer farmer and did much to stamp out TB in cattle; also he had an inexhaustible knowledge of wild life and local history going back to Roman times. When he said he could walk on heather from his house to the North Sea, I am sure it was so. He had a rugged face with clear blue eyes and the most beautiful deep rumbling voice, rich and slow with the true Lancashire burr.

Ken, the second brother, was named John Kenyon, after Grandpapa, just as Wyn had been named after our other Grandpapa Edwin Henry. The third brother was christened Frederic Phillips and called Eric (because of Uncle Fred); it was very confusing for people outside the family. Later they added to the confusion by marrying a Cicely and two Phyllises.

Wyn was a Kenyon in build, quick-witted and with a good eye. Games were easy for him and he could do conjuring tricks with billiard balls or coins or balance things on his nose whilst walking round the room, deeds that held us young ones spellbound so that now, nearly thirty years after his death, middle-aged people recall his magic and charm. He did not miss a chance to tease. Connie, always deadly serious about herself, was easy prey. She would slowly, carefully, choose the best of the dates from the box, only to find that by some sleight of hand he had removed them from her plate, at which Mother would shake her head gently, saying, "Wyn dear, you shouldn't," and Connie would storm while we younger ones grinned.

Ken was shy and thoughtful, playing with me when I was small and later aware of my loneliness, as no-one else was, least of all myself. He would buy me books on birds and Viking sagas. He also gave me two guinea pigs, which I am sorry to say I neglected, being by that time withdrawn into a happy, slightly melancholy world, singing away on my swing as I watched the sunset. Trudging about with a water bottle and staff, being a Palmer, or getting from one place to another unseen as a skulking Jacobite. Not doing anything in particular but being somebody or other, not myself. The world was a far away place connected with the inability to spell, and those long earnest talks about being good, that brought on passionate fits of crying, which bewildered my governess and me. One must be good; there were all those bits in the Bible about buried talents and the foolish virgins, and I was not good. "You must go to your room and think about it and then come and say you are sorry. That means you are truly sorry and will never do it again." Knowing enough of human nature even at that age, I knew it wasn't possible, so I wrote myself off. Perhaps I was a miserable sinner.

After Ken, came Eric who had tubercular trouble, always wearing a bandage and soft scarf round his throat. He suffered badly at his spartan school and at 17 went to Edinburgh, where he had the most extensive operation on his neck and shoulder performed at that time. After a long weary convalescence, he went to live on several farms, as he needed an outdoor life and farming was what he wanted to do.

Cicely followed at the usual two-year gap. When young, she prayed hard to be a boy and wore the most boyish clothes permissible, a kilted

In the Study

A long earnest talk about being good.

skirt and jersey. I have a snapshot memory of her having a violent fight on the landing when somebody wished to tie a large bow on her head when she was dressed for a party. Having once been sick in the carriage with Grandmama, she rode on the box, sitting very straight with arms folded, hoping she would be mistaken for a footman. Later there was much concern about her back. Spines were very much on grown-up's minds then, and later at school, health inspection consisted on looking at tonsils (and being prescribed a daily painting of them with iodine) and a chilly business when, stripped to the waist, people marked the knobs of your vertebrae with a pencil and then stood back to see if they were in line. Cicely's knobs cannot have been, as she was taken to see a great man in Liverpool. After that she did some of her lessons on an inclined board with a bar for the feet and a hole for the back of the head. Also a trapeze was fixed up in a back bedroom. This was fun. I cannot remember any remedial exercises, nor did we teach ourselves to be trapeze artists, but you could stand or hang upside down and swing on it, so long as you didn't come off and land in the fire grate.

Cicely followed Connie to the school in Scotland. It had been run by Miss Henrietta Jex-Blake, and was a happy place. Unfortunately, on Miss Jex-Blake's becoming Mistress of Lady Margaret Hall a woman came who, though a mathematician, should never have taken up teaching, let alone being a headmistress. Some genius at the school she had left had nicknamed her The Cold Poached Egg. I should pity her, I know, and I try to, for her endless demand for more Esprit de Corps. She never realised that she had achieved it by making her girls so unhappy that they were particularly nice to each other. They were all a very nice lot, as were the staff with two exceptions, but when I followed Cicely some years later, when she was head girl, we all lived under a thundercloud that frequently broke in terrible inexplicable rows. Cicely, honest and over-conscientious, got the worst of it. In boys' schools it might have been beatings, but physical punishment, even if unjust, has not the lasting effect of mental and emotional violence.

There was a custom that if an old girl gained an academic honour the school had a holiday. One day it was announced at prayers, that this had happened, so we should have our holiday on Saturday (already a half day) and the morning would be spent carrying benches and chairs down to the cricket field. The enormity of this swindle struck Cicely dumb, so that she did not call for three rapturous cheers. Black gloom swamped us. There was an interview in the Head's holy of holies, a room garnished with monstrous pot cats with long necks and glass eyes. It went on so long that poor Cicely, one of the bravest people I know, lost her nerve and apologised, a thing she regretted for the rest of her life.

I went there when I was nearly twelve years old. Apart from long division and poetry, I arrived practically uneducated. It was odd being English. Heather did not grow south of the border, and we were a decadent race, putting sugar on its porridge. Good training to be in a minority and take the teasing, and the incontrovertible fact that Scotland was superior. It made me realise that we English can be sloppy thinkers when our havering is pulled up by an earnest stare and the words, "Is that a faact?" This exactitude gives pleasure, when across the border, to see the sign: 'Aereated Drinks' instead of our dotty English: 'Mineral Waters,' which suggests we might want a pint of iron filings. Also when you ask the way there is no vagueness ending in those improbable words: "You can't go wrong." Instead you enter into a serious consultation considering the merits of various routes. Never the despairing cry of the Irishman: "If I was going to Roscommon, I wouldn't be starting from here!"

Also it makes me realise that we English must madden everyone else, because we do not need to tell people we are superior.

Before my schooldays we went to Switzerland for the sports. Winter sports were still in their infancy, no ski lifts or even seal-skins to help you climb, or icy tracks and struggles to attain stars for merit. The mornings were spent zig-zagging up to the high snow, eating our packed lunch on the sunny side of a chalet and then coming down through soft unscarred snow. The telemark was the only turn used. Bob-sleighs ran on the road, where the bends were banked up high and men were posted at intervals to blow on cowhorns to clear the track, and of course, there was a flooded ice-rink with a part set aside for curling.

Females wore puttees on their legs and tweed breeches, and the grown-ups wore skirts down the ankles, knitted jackets and flannel hoods. There was no long boring *apres ski* period. After a superb tea, people changed, dined and then danced, had fancy dress carnivals and competitions. Our hotel was a really old wooden building full of fretwork, Victorian furniture and books telling of the sufferings of the Huguenots. Father's sisters had visited it when they were schoolgirls in the early 1880s.

The journey was adventurous. Luckily, I was a good sailor and could appreciate the luncheon baskets waiting in our railway carriage at Calais. Then dinner at the Gare de l'Est and the long uncomfortable night sitting up in the carriage, as we never ran to sleepers, and I doubt if there were any on the train. In the morning the meticulously tidy Swiss stations with breakfast of croissants and black cherry jam, and the excitement of having to crane your neck to see the snowy mountain tops. At Aigle we got into a Diligence - hard mustard-coloured seats, the luggage on top, drawn by four stout horses. We left the Rhone Valley and plodded up to a small town where, after lunch, we changed into gorgeous sleighs pulled by pairs of horses decked with feathers and bells.

The second year we went on to Italy. Not arranged beforehand, we took it in easy stages, staying in small old-fashioned hotels. Milan was our first stop. We were high up over a narrow shopping street, when we heard the lovely heart-rending sound of Chopin's *Funeral March*, as a procession passed below us. Italy was mourning her soldiers fallen in the War in Tripoli. I had not known there was a war so this was strange and new. This was not like those pictures in the *Illustrated London News*. This was sorrow. It has echoed in my ears ever since.

Eleven years old is a good time for sight-seeing. All that gazing and dreaming had given me visual awareness, so that things I saw then have been especially clear and real. Boticelli's Venus was a glorious discovery and the next time I was in Florence I hastened to revisit her as a dear friend. She is just as lovely, but she does not make me want to shout as she did then.

It was early spring so there was no throng of tourists. In Venice the gondolas were the usual way of getting about. Our hotel there, and in Florence, had been the palaces of rich merchants. Warren-like buildings where you could lie in bed admiring your ceiling, where painted balustrades led your eyes to a blue sky with roses and birds and possibly a cupid. How I wish I could find a room in the Ufizzi where the wall panels opened to show on the inner sides most marvellous maps where sea monsters, mermen and galleons swam. Rome has few memories because I was in bed for most of the time, but what charmed me was that level with my room, across the street, was a complete village of small roof-top buildings crowded with jolly Italian families, flowers in tubs, washing and poultry. There they were in the sun, with the clanging rushing city far below.

Then waking in Naples to see a lemon tree full of fruit and flowers outside my windows! The desolation of Pompeii: two stallions harnessed each to a calash, rearing and screaming as they fought. The hordes of beggars showing their deformities at the quayside when we embarked for the 24-hour long voyage up to Genoa. The ship was a very grand German liner, all bobble-edged curtains, violin music and mountains of food, Teutonic grandeur laid on thick.

The most memorable thing for me in Genoa was the Campo Santo, where the heirs of Leonardo da Vinci had carved complete family groups. There sat Mama in her cap and bustle, busy crocheting, whilst Papa read the paper and the rest of the family grouped themselves round the table, with its cloth and aspidistra. The dottiest was a memorial showing two gentlemen, who had managed to reach the next world in full nineteenth century costume; waving their bowler hats, they rushed to embrace.

Reading was now gripping me: Conan Doyle's historical stories, Kipling and Stevenson, whose nostalgia answered my homesickness when at school. The best part of being at school was the first morning at home - getting outside at six or earlier to walk barefoot through the wet grass, or later to sit in a warm hideout on the garden wall reading Henty. I didn't learn much about the campaigns but gloried in the names - Salamanca, Badajoz, Corruna.

I think it was four years earlier when motoring was still an adventure that we took our holiday in Wales. The first time we broke our journey at Pentre Voelis. Here the hotel was full so we slept over the village shop. The good lady asked if I was frightened by the noise, which was the very best thing about the place. It was a delight. The smell of roasting coffee filled the room as I lay listening to the vivacious Welsh conversation. Next morning there was the homely clash of milk pails and clucking hens. I slipped into my clothes and was away downstairs and across the dusty white road, climbing over a gate into a little meadow. The long grass was full of scabious, wine red burnet and potentillas. Across it a tiny stream chuckled over rocks as it dashed to meet the Conway far below in the woods. From the mountains came a soft wind scented with bog myrtle. That morning there was something there far richer and more blissful than anything in this world. It was my first experience of ecstasy. In spite of many times of joy and beauty, I doubt if I shall meet it again.

I made a pilgrimage to that meadow not so long ago. It is unaltered and a very lovely spot. The holiness is a treasure stored in the heart forever.

CHAPTER 3

School Years

Then came the long hot summer of 1914, a year forever set to
music of the two waltzes, *Destiny* and *The Druid's Prayer*, slow
sorrowful tunes, which were the rage, and to which we danced
in the big dining-room. Our vicar exchanged parishes with another
man who had two splendid handsome sons, who would come over for
tennis. One evening we watched fascinated as a battery of horse-drawn
artillery came jingling over the grass, to a quiet bend of the brook
sheltered by the woods. Tents went up and the horses were picketted
in long lines whilst the officers strolled up to the house to dine with
us. They were Territorials and kindly told the kid sister the meaning of
Ubique on their badge. It must have been early in July for there was no
talk of war as far as I can remember. They left next morning at dawn,
only the long lines of crushed grass and steaming dung showing where
they had camped.

They passed, just as the Scots did in 1647, 1715 and later in 1945,
and who may well have chosen that very spot to bivouac. Our parish
was full of memories of ambush, escape and of men being paid off at
the White Horse after the Civil War, so they too, with the rumble and
jingle of the guns, passed, and our tennis players went in their turn.

A short time later there was a serious tenseness in the house. Wyn
was going into camp earlier, and this time in the big public hall in the
town. Mother was contriving a sleeping bag out of blankets, and soon
he had his marching orders to go south to guard railways until the
time came to join the British Expeditionary Force (BEF) in France.

45

I had left the school in Scotland and was now to go to Godstowe at High Wycombe, a good school where the top storey was filled with looms, a book-binding bench and a studio. The teaching was good. Two elderly sisters, with high starched collars and tight belts, into which they would push their gold watches tethered by long chains round their necks, made history come alive, and even gave me a faint acquaintance with the theory of music.

English grammar was totally incomprehensible - why do teachers fail to explain those long strange words never met outside the classroom? Attempts at parsing must have been as bewildering to them as it was to me because I stuck these words at random into various sections of the ruled page, hoping that the hundred to one gamble might come off. As for Latin, it became a blank. My teacher was so exasperated that she told me I was mentally deficient. Had I had more pluck I should have shown her that I was not. Instead I accepted the fact and ceased to make any effort. When in 1916 I went to St Felix in Southwold, I thought that they would find this out soon enough, and so wasted my schooling years.

I must have been seedy as I had a term off school, staying in Wales and then St Felix was chosen as having good sea air, in place of Wycombe Abbey, which stands in a rather dank valley. Why the sea air, which howls down on the Suffolk coast, should be superior, instead of some place nearer Lancashire, I do not know. Somebody had told my parents about the excellent headmistress, Miss Silcox. No-one thought about the geography. It was about as far from home as could be. Getting there entailed crossing over London and with the war on there was the bother of getting someone to see me across to Liverpool Street. Then our train might be held up for hours while Red Cross trains passed through, and at Hailsworth we changed into the collection of very old carriages and a little engine chuffed and wobbled for the last ten miles.

I think that both Father and Mother knew little about schools. Mother had been to a day school run by very cultured German ladies in Manchester, and Father had only had a short period at Arnold House in quiet little Blackpool. A good thing was that, perhaps because of the war, there were no exeats at half term, when being so far from home would have made me miserable. A cousin did look me up, resplendent in uniform and on a horse, which reminds me that a year before, at Godstowe, a girl of eleven had the delight of being taken out by her nephew, a major in the army.

Having thrown in my hand at learning, I got little of it. Hating crowds thoroughly, I made no friends, so must have been an awkward cuss to everyone. Fortunately, there was a remarkable woman who taught singing. She had me doing breath control exercises and singing scales and long passages on a rolled R. This pitches your voice into the back of your nose and controls your diaphragm so that years later a rather drunk friend said, "Y'know the thing about Joan is that she never breathes," which showed I had learnt something.

Also, bless her, there was Ma Becker, and sometimes Pa, in charge of painting, both of whom were gifted teachers, who would say, "Paint what you see, not what you know," in other words, nothing should be painted according to a recipe.

In those days St Felix was noted for being dead set on deportment. There were to be no slouching girls, so we competed for a shield to be won by the house that collected the fewest marks! The gym mistress would prowl about giving them out should she catch anyone with the elbow on a desk, and each term houses would go over to the school and process along the corridors and up and down the stairs with books on girls' heads, in the manner of African porters. If you weren't good at this, house prefects got you up early and made you practise up and down your own house. Boring it was, but I note that elderly Feliciana retain straight backs.

I went to the school in the spring of 1916, after it had returned to its own buildings. It had roved about since 1914 when Scarborough was shelled and the girls' school there moved to a safer place. This early attempt at what was to be known as Evacuation proved so dismal that, very depleted in numbers, it returned to Southwold. That term we had our bombardment, as well as several air raids. Shells landed very close indeed! We girls were thrilled. Not so the staff, but the school stayed on and apart from alarms we were never hit. We thought it fun, too, when we bicycled to see the skeleton of a Zeppelin, which had come down in flames, with no thought for the crew.

While at St Margaret's school in Scotland, I had developed blinding headaches, not, I think, true migraines; they continued until I was in my thirties. Quite often they were not so very bad, but, loathing games, I dishonestly made the most of them to get out of pounding up and down after a ball.

Of preparation for Confirmation I remember nothing at all, except that we would go on Sunday afternoons to recite the Catechism to the Headmistress. We were so earnest about it and terrified that someone might say she would keep their hands from sticking and peeling, that of course a wretched girl did and dissolved in tears. I missed the school service by having German measles and so was 'done' later in the term at Bungay, or maybe Beccles, with a crowd of strangers. The parents came down for the occasion. The extra coaching I had I have also forgotten; my only reaction was a conviction that I was one with all people everywhere. This did not make me any less a loner.

There were long, long pi-jaws. Being quite ignorant of sex and the way of the world, I had not the foggiest idea what the pi-jawer was going on about. Sometimes it would be said that something was to be avoided because it was 'suggestive.' I disconcerted the speaker by asking what it was suggesting. I think the answer was 'unpleasantness,' or something equally vague, so <u>that</u> didn't enlighten me. Our house-mistress was especially earnest, indeed she thought that to sing a hymn tune when running about the house was very wrong, probably blasphemous, and warranted a solemn reproach. As for crushes, they were silly and incomprehensible and very mild. Somebody might be said to be agog for some hero in the first eleven, but there did not seem to be any signs of love; it was far easier to be in love with heroes in history or novels.

When Wyn's battalion was practically wiped out on June 15th at Festubert, Mother had woken and said to Father, "Wyn is in deadly danger, but he will be alright." They left a huge gap into which all the other casualty lists fell, putting finality to thoughts of future love.

Home life went on quietly. Rations were not as well organised as they were in the next war, but being in the country we had eggs and a pig to salt down. Also, a kind farmer would pop a pound of butter into our pew on a Sunday. Ken went into the Royal Flying Corps (RFC), so Father had to work very hard. Eric managed a farm in East Lothian, where he would have almost starved if the cook had not fortified him with glasses of milk. She followed him south when he left, so we acquired 'wee Aag,' a tiny person, who had the gift of restoring life to the most wilted plant or young chicken in no time at all. Eric then went to Lincolnshire, after having another operation on his glands, where he supervised flax-growing for the Government. In those days Scunthorpe was a remote place where old memories hung on. There had been fights between the fenmen and the Dutch, who were brought over to drain the land in the 1600s. The river had been diverted on a straight course out to sea, leaving a winding green strip where it had previously flowed. Eric met a neighbour who looked so black with anger that he asked him what was up. Pointing to this width of grass, he growled that his son was courting a bitch from across the water.

It was in 1915 that our vicar heard about one of the parishioners grumbling about the state of the land, now Crown property. It was not like the old days, but Old Squire died and Young Squire, "We heard nothing of him." The Scots, he said, "Wished to be friendly but, remembering older times, they took no chances, cutting cavities in the haystacks where they hid their horses. They took nowt but the Father's clogs, and the lad as took them threw them back up the loan and sez, 'Ah canna walk in wooden shoon.' But eh, poor lads, you couldn't but be sorry for them when they came back." He was talking about 1715.

We would spend our holidays at Shap Wells, a small hotel lost in a sea of heather, with two tumbling becks and a sulphur well giving off a powerful smell of rotten eggs. The family had stayed there in the 1890s when the proprietress made marvelous meringues and the head-waiter kept a beetle in a matchbox - two legends passed down to me. Even without meringues or beetles it was a heavenly place, though some people would stare around with amazement asking what on earth was there to do.

On birthdays at home we would entertain old dug-outs from Preston Barracks. One, the son of a parson, had got a commission in the 11th Hussars, becoming a bear-leader to the eldest son of the Prince of Wales. Known as Prince Collar and Cuffs, to the great benefit of the nation, he died young, leaving his brother to become King George V. An amusing old chap, a Knight of Windsor, Major P would ask my Mother if, as an old man with a very shaky hand, he might have his wine in the water goblet, which held quite three times as much as the correct glass. The other dug-out was a gentleman in a humble county regiment. Once he let out that he made it a rule that wherever he was staying, be it mansion or hotel, he made his bed on a Sunday. This does not make the terrific impact it did then, when it was a kindness and courtesy almost reaching eccentricity.

Another younger man came driving a smart Stanhope and pair. An interesting type, very handsome save for a flattened nose; he had, he said, sailed before the mast, ranched cattle and had adventures all over the world. He charmed us like Othello, though I doubt whether all his stories were true. Cicely couldn't bear him. I worshipped; I think Mother did a bit too and he had a very brief engagement to Connie. Eventually he returned to the front, writing grim, witty letters for a while. We did not see his name in the casualty lists, so I suppose he must have moved on to fresh fields on which to play his game of make-believe.

Before the war we would be visited by a real veteran called George Smith. He spent the summer at an hotel opposite the Barracks gates. He had been with the little band who held the ford at Rourke's Drift in 1879, that desperate stand saving Natal from massacre by the spears of Cetawayo's Zulu Impi. Had he not been a clergyman he would have been awarded the ninth Victoria Cross (VC) to the eight that were given. As it was, he handed out the ammunition and tended the wounded. The Zulus charged and charged again until their dead lay level with the parapet of sacks, stores and brushwood, while the building went up in flames. He said his little dog died there standing guard over its master's kit. Although a Hero, he was not on my list of the worshipped. He told alarming stories and had a huge bristly beard and tickled me.

The war ended when the school was in the middle of the terrible flu epidemic. No one died at St Felix, but we were too groggy to appreciate what was happening. The next summer I left feeling guilty because I was beside myself with joy when all the other leavers were correctly heart-broken. My house-mistress staggered me by saying that if I took up writing she would be interested to see my work. I still wonder why she did not say that two years earlier; I never got anything more than an occasional 'Good' and had to spend most of my prep writing out dozens of spelling mistakes three times, a task which made not the slightest improvement.

I wonder whether it would have helped if we were told to write half a page on a subject and look up every word in the dictionary? The trouble is that if you are a colossally bad speller, it is almost impossible to find the word in the dictionary, a thing good spellers do not understand. Samuel Johnson did us a disservice by standardising the spelling of the English language. Before that even lawyers and bishops spelt as they felt, making words gloriously forceful and jolly. That was that.

Anyway, I am sure young people need praise. It makes you humble and happy, not bumptious. I nearly fell off my bike when I heard a woman say, "That girl has a nice face," a remark which set me up for years and still comes back with a glow of gratitude. I thought myself a clumsy oaf. Young people are self-centred unless they are abnormally good. I haven't met one yet. On the other hand, if you are told you are a chump or a vandal, you will probably accept the fact, and become one. There is nothing so hopeless as the desperation of the young.

After a very strenuous term at a Domestic Economy School, set in the lovely Malvern Hills, I looked round for something to do. Cicely had been working as a secretary at the War Office after coming down from Oxford. She was going to London to polish up her typing and shorthand. I did not think I was good enough to take up art, (though I think I could have been good as an illustrator), so thought my interest in faces could be put to use in photography. I should have gone to a technical college, and also learnt somehow to deal with people. Instead I went as an apprentice to Walter Barnett's photographic studio in Knightsbridge. He was a real artist and stories were told how he would bellow at some very grand starchy woman until she wept or flew into a rage, whereupon he would say, "There, now, you've relaxed so we can make a real picture of you." Unfortunately, he had just sold the business to a man less gifted, who thought people wished to look like stiff pot dolls. There was a war between him and the dear old retoucher, who removed blemishes from negatives but left the modelling and character there. It was interesting to work with a fine scalpel on the negatives. We might be asked to change a hair style, put in an engagement ring, and of course, remove every crease from a uniform and many pounds of flesh from the neck and shoulders of the sitter.

It was an enjoyable time and fun when there was a levee or court clients coming in uniform, or gowns with trains and the required three white ostrich feathers in their hair. One day Ellen Terry came and I missed seeing her, but I had the privilege of hearing her voice. She was asking for a cab and it was golden music.

Cicely and I had two rooms in the Fulham area. I cannot remember what we paid for them, plus breakfast and supper. It was very little. Those were the days when you could get a good two-course meal for one shilling and sixpence. Lunch at Harrods was half a crown, and a superbly grand lunch with an orchestra at the Trocadero cost three and sixpence. You could pay five pounds for a pretty lacy dance frock, maybe a pound more if it was made for you, and 'undies' and blouses were of crepe de chine, real silk and very much warmer than the despised artificial stuff. A few years later I had a suit made for me by a famous tailor in the north. He charged the staggering price of fourteen pounds, two pounds less than the Queen's tailor charged. For it I got a coat and skirt in fine West of England suiting. It had a line of blue running through it so the lining of real silk had blue binding at the edges, also two crepe de chine blouses to match, mostly made by hand, plus two ties and silk handkerchiefs with my initials embroidered on them. After six years' hard wear, I gave the suit away as I was tired of it, but it looked as good as new.

Our favourite theatre was the Old Vic, nearly in Waterloo Station and run by Miss Lillian Bayliss. Stalls cost a shilling, other seats only fourpence or twopence, but we chose to be grand. We saw Shakespeare and grand opera, the costumes reappearing, perhaps slightly altered, week after week, which didn't bother anyone, any more than that the scenery was ply-wood and clever lighting. Miss Bayliss had run the place as a Coffee Ball with entertainment thrown in, as an alternative to the pubs. It was said that she ran it on a strange belief in Guidance, and would demand that God would send her plenty of young men – "and see that they can act," which he did. It went in for lectures, teetotal meetings and the embryo Morley College, under the guidance of her Aunt, Miss Emma Cone. Never in debt, it reeled along on a few hundred pounds, and every conceivable difficulty. Not the least being that actors and orchestra had practically no time to rehearse, so odd things could happen. In *Figaro* when the Countess and Susanna stripped Cherubino's coat off, she was without a shirt wearing a very up-to-date cammie and a gold slave bangle, whereon all three got the giggles, as did the audience.

The most memorable production for me was *Peer Gynt* with Russell Thorndike in the lead, and Edvard Grieg's music. Since then I have heard several versions on the radio with varying cuts and new music, but nothing coming near the effect got from colour wed to this music. I find it odd to bring in the madhouse scene and leave out the kernel of the play, which is surely the logical, frightening interview with the button moulder, and how I missed the last gentle notes of Solvig's lullaby, which ends the ghastly pilgrimage in beauty.

Another play I was privileged to see in the West End was *Cyrano de Bergerac*, played by Robert Loraine, the scenery by Edmund Dulac. This was as rich and elaborate as the Old Vic was spartan, and the very peak of high romance. Also a band of Russian refugees were putting on the *Chauve Souris*, each little scene a jewel of silliness, beauty or roaring Russian gusto.

To get back to prices. Life has changed and we oldies show signs of shock at the cost of things in the 1970s. I do not think the reason things were cheap was because wages were unjustly low. They may have been in some cases. For instance, at the beginning of the century you could buy a rather nasty fumed oak bedroom suite, including wardrobe and washstand, for five pounds. My old friend, the retoucher of photographs, was one of a big family where the father, who drove drays, got 22 shillings a week. The mother, a good housekeeper, fed them well. In the 1920s an excellent cookery book came out, written for the young wives of professional men, showing how you could feed a family at 10 shillings a head per week, on a good middle-class diet, not pig's trotters and tripe. The people who did feel the pinch were the clergy. They went in for large families and were expected to keep up with the gentry. Many had an income of less than 300 pounds a year. A clergy-daughter admitted that the first new garment she possessed was at 18 years old; all before had been cast-offs.

It was surprising what could be bought for a shilling. Hard-backed red Nelson classics with an illustrated front piece, linen handkerchiefs, man's silk ties - I could get Christmas presents for the eight of us out of the golden half sovereign given me for this delightful task, then a little girl.

The food we ate was staggering. Possibly the helpings were smaller, though I doubt it. Although we weren't well off, our good middle-class meals included game and salmon and superb grapes, though these were often sent by friends. Our Sunday fare went like this: breakfast at nine o'clock was porridge or grapenuts. (I don't know why we were so loyal to the last. Cousins seemed to have other cereals but grapenuts it was for us). Sausages and bacon followed like night and day. Toast and marmalade, of course, and coffee. Back from church and hungry, we attacked soup, sometimes artichoke, thick, creamy and I thought horrid. Then a vast sirloin. Along with the beef was light puffy Yorkshire pudding, roast potatoes and some green vegetable, followed by a trifle made as Mrs Beeton instructs, ox in summer and, best of all, blackberry pudding. After the pudding came Lancashire cheese, butter and Huntly & Palmar's rusks. Again, we were conservatives so that we hardly knew there were other biscuits. Then the table was solemnly cleared of crumbs and silver and the dessert service with a pretty mat and finger-bowl to each plate set out. (You could play tunes by rubbing your finger round the glass bowls until told to stop) and an array of fruits and nuts finished the meal.

It was grand because it was Sunday and the whole family sat together along with a guest or two. At five we sat round the big table again for tea, unlike other days when a small table in the drawing room or billiard room was used. A big table was useful as there were a lot of us and there was jam, honey and, at Christmas, preserved ginger along with the scones and cakes. The only thing that marred it for me, when we were young, was that Father would try out our mental arithmetic, making it Sunday-ish by saying, "I went to Mr Platt's and bought three Bibles and four hymn books," at various prices. These difficult mathematics were far beyond me and put my head in a whirl. The others, being practically grown up, got the answers almost instantly. Then as the maids had the evening free so that they could go to church, we had a light supper. There would be a hot dish of something or other, and cold meats, salad and a cold pudding. It has just occurred to me that I don't believe we washed up afterwards, so someone must have stayed on duty and had extra work to do. This has given me quite a shock!

CHAPTER 4

Eric Moves to Kenya

In 1919 Wyn married, setting up house in St Annes. The next year Eric sailed for Kenya. British East Africa, as it was called then, was developing after the war, and a scheme was drawn up to grow flax in an uninhabited stretch of land near Gilgil. Eric, with his knowledge of flax growing and retting, went to have a look at it. By the time he arrived the scheme had collapsed, with only the stone-built manager's houses to show where it was to have been. (The largest house is now Pembroke House School).

Eric went on safari with a government official with whom he had made friends on the voyage, an elderly Highlander whose job was to inspect prisons. He lived in a thick haze of whisky, but he was held in great affection by the African police and prisoners as well as chiefs.

After this, Eric travelled up to Laikipia with a man who had a car. It broke down and for three days they lived off a kongoni they had shot, until a man, who had gone back for a spare part, returned. Then they pushed on to Rumuruti and out to the Pesi River. Laikipia is a large district stretching from the Aberdare Mountains to Mount Kenya. Watered by a few rivers, which join the Ewaso Ngiro. It is for the most part rolling grassland sprinkled with the flat-topped thorn trees.

Years back the Maasai had lived here raiding the Kikuyu tribe who lived in the forests to the south. They were moved to join the rest of their people in the huge area on the Kenya-Tanganyika border. Now it had been surveyed and divided into areas averaging 6,000 acres or so. The boundaries of these farms-to-be were marked by pieces of railway

Eric Booth sailed for Kenya in 1920.

line set in a lump of concrete. With only a blueprint and compass, the purchaser had a hard time finding these markers, especially since the grass was long, or an elephant, having stubbed its foot on the iron, had pulled it out.

Quite a number of these plots were bought at a very low price by ex-service men, some of whom got their homes built only to discover the houses were not on their land. But mud and wattle thatched buildings go up quickly, so after groping about a bit they got themselves established. There were no fences. The Public Works Department (PWD) had made culverts and wooden bridges on the earth track, which ran from Gilgil to Rumuruti and on to Nyeri. These last places had District Commissioners, police posts, stores and post offices. Nyeri even had a hotel and a prison – 'Hotel ya Kingi Georgi' – where you got meat to eat.

Lion and leopard abounded so cattle were guarded by herdsmen and, at night, enclosed in a boma where a fire burnt by the gate. A lion can jump a six-foot fence, hauling a well-grown heifer out with the ease of a dog with a hare. At other times the pride would roar, trying to stampede the herd into breaking out.

Eric's choice of farm was roughly triangular, on the Pesi swamp, a large area of papyrus inhabited by plenty of hippo and waterbuck and edged by tall lemon-barked acacias. It was too far from water for cattle to graze the back of the farm, so years passed before a bore hole pumped water up into dams built to conserve it in the river bed of the Marogo, which formerly only ran for a few months in the year. At the time of Eric's death this was accomplished and now there is a small lake abounding in water fowl and a permanent stream, which is something very good to leave behind you.

Eric's first night on the farm was much interrupted. His mongrel dog kept crawling into the tent under his camp bed. After several of these disturbances, Eric took the dog by the scruff of the neck, opened the flap and found himself handing it to a lion. Sitting on his bed with his gun on his knees, he waited until the moon rose, when he shot the lion at a few yards range. The whole pride roared for the rest of the night. When dawn came he found the dead lion nearby. The dog surprisingly recovered.

After this he built a small square hut - the usual wattle and daub thatched affair - with a window and a door made from some planks with bits of rawhide for hinges. Nearby a kitchen hut had one wall of stones against which was the fire. Cooking pots balanced on stones and that useful tin container – a debe – served as the oven, nestled in the wood ash. Another hut without the daub on the walls made a dairy and the cattle he bought were boma'd a short way away where the labour lived in their round huts. Then he began to build a real house with a living room, store, bathroom, and two bedrooms; it was to have two bay windows, a very high-pitched thatched roof and cedar slab walls. This wood was fetched by oxcart from the sawmills 30 miles away.

He had gone into partnership with his neighbour, David Flett, a true Orcadian – not a Scot as he would point out. In 1922 when Eric sailed for England, he left David to see that the house was completed, David having already finished building his own.

The reason for his returning home was that it was the Guild Year when all Prestonians return if they possibly can. It was decided after

58

Robert the Bruce burnt the town down that the guilds would have a special Festival every twenty years, and as far as I know only Hitler postponed one. It lasts a week and after the hereditary Freeman have registered their presence and nominated their sons, there begins every sort of festivity, pageant, concert, ball, agricultural and industrial show and of course, processions. We are keen on processions in the north; even the depressions of the 1930s did not stop every union and church getting going with banners and, if possible, new clothes at Whitsuntide.

That winter we three sisters had gone again to Las Diablerets for winter sports. Now after the war we could dare to wear breeches and knee length coats for skiing. Afterwards we joined the parents at Rapallo, then a quiet place where large numbers of retired clergy lived frugally. They seemed to be all in their eighties, thinking nothing of taking their packed lunches and fairly scampering up and down those steep little mountains, one having five hundred steps. Evenings were spent playing Hearts, a card game considered to be less worldly than Bridge, though actually far more malicious, and Sunday evenings were given over to tremendous hymn singing.

There was a delightful old Admiral there. He told us that he had been brought up in Jamaica, and at five years old it was his great pleasure to listen to a very old African lady who was well into her 90s. She had told him how, as a young woman, she had been the head wife of a great chief; but after a terrible tribal war she had been sold and shipped to the West Indies. He never forgot her and her stories, so when a grown man he studied the history of the West Coast. Sure enough, he found that the Ibo and Yoruba in Nigeria had had a particularly savage war in the 1790s, fitting in with the old lady's age.

After the Guild, when Eric was due to sail for Kenya, he suggested that Cicely and I should go back with him. The wonderful country, with its superb climate, where you are on the Equator at an altitude of 6,000 feet, appealed to us. He thought his house should be finished, and we should have the company of David Flett's fiancée, who was leaving her home in Edinburgh to marry him.

We sailed from Tilbury in the *Llanstephen Castle*. "What a

marvelous time you will have," said the Aunts, and I longed to be a raging success instead of the headache-ridden bottled-up person, always a wallflower at dances. Some time before this I had read that shyness was really selfishness. The article was illustrated by a picture of a man and woman each surrounded by a large fog shaped like themselves. This made me angry because I knew it to be true. All those helpful talks, all the urging to be good, tidy, amusing and helpful were a burden. "You will always be one of a crowd. There's no such thing as a private life." This advice made me long for a desert island. Apart from large red spots, which blotched my face whenever there was a dance or party, I wasn't bad looking, and had a good singing voice but there was a cringing fear between me and real living:

O Lord, forgive
That we have traded in the second best,
This shoddy work, the lust
For quiet, for rest.
O Lord! Forgive!
Like things that crawl away
From brightness, of your day
Seeking some darker spot,
Complaining of our lot
For fear of Your bright ray.
Oh, turn me to the sun,
So that my body glows
And my weak spirit knows
The brilliance of Your Son.
Then finds its loyalty
To the transforming Love,
That strangely from above
In wonder, comes to me.

That was the thing I could not find, though I saw it in my parents. I envied those people who showed bouncing self-confidence, but I was back on to those books about a devout life, which seemed made out of courage, discipline and drudgery. That drove me further into my private funk-hole, where I could daydream about romantic heroism.

It had been about that time that our vicar, taking it for granted that as I came from a good home I would be automatically adequate, tried to rope me into teaching in Sunday School. On opening the book of lessons he gave me, the first question was, "What is Grace?" Knowing well that I had not the foggiest idea, I closed the book and opted out of the job, never telling him why – a bit of bad manners of which I am ashamed.

CHAPTER 5

Arrival at Rumuruti

Now here was a door opening from my protected life out into a new world. Before sailing there was the business of collecting things needed to set up house and to review our clothes. We knew there would be dust and heat and were told that practically everything that grew in Africa had thorns, sharp hooks or sharp pointed seeds, so we collected the clothes landgirls had worn, breeches, boys' woollen stockings, stout shoes and socks. Trousers or shorts were, as yet, unthought of. Everybody believed it was certain death to go outside bareheaded between eight in the morning until four in the afternoon, so we must have topees, and those double felt hats known as terais. The usual thing was to get these at Port Said. It was said that harmful rays could strike through one's back, affecting the spinal cord, and so we should have spine pads – T-shaped thick things made of khaki and red cloth, buttoning across the shoulders. Also you could get suits or shirts of safari cloth, woven one side khaki and the other scarlet. Frocks were worn on social occasions, for tennis, or when in Nairobi. Gloves, long ones, were only needed when visiting Government House. An Aunt, who had travelled quite a bit, insisted on our having woolen cholera belts. The only time they might have been useful was in the Red Sea when we lay on our bunks in the sweltering heat with the fan directed on us, but we did not think of it at the time and got the usual upset insides. There were also soft knee-high mosquito boots for the evenings.

The same Aunt provided us with a most curious sauce-boat-shaped object made of grey rubber. How she found it I do not know unless the Army and Navy Stores stocked it. It was a traveller's – a lady traveller's – chamber pot. We thought it the crowning piece of our equipment, but at times we found it useful. We went to Gammage's. It is a pity I did not keep the bills. There was china, or rather pot, for the house and aluminium for safari. Cretonne at a shilling a yard, camp beds and those large holdalls into which they went along with bedding, saddles and fishing rods and guns. By great good luck I found in an old established ironmonger's shop in Preston, an oval bath, cream within, painted like grained wood. It had a lid held on with a strap. It was the kind of thing Victorian families would take to seaside lodgings and a blessing it was, as an extra trunk, reverting to its duty as our bath when we arrived. Wyn let us have his camp chest of drawers that packed into a large box with hinged doors. It would obviously make a superb sideboard.

Then at a very shabby, <u>very</u> superior gunsmiths in London, Eric bought a small automatic for desperate occasions, and on asking for a simple shot-gun an extremely ancient man, wearing a skull cap, crept up from below with a twelve-bore single-barrelled Martini. It was a bit of a curiosity as to load you yanked an iron lever down, (it did not break at the breech) and shoved your cartridge in and brought the lever up. It was the same mechanism as the guns used in the army before the repeater rifle was invented and why it was in existence beats me. But it worked and the idea was that you carried some number five when looking for birds, keeping a few SSG or even a ball cartridge for any big game, should it turn nasty. It was well this never happened, as I am incurably gun-shy, leaping in the air as I press the trigger. The gun came into use later for setting lion traps, when it was wired to a double barred opening into a boma built round a dead beast. A wire was attached to the trigger and down to the ground. When the animal put its head in the gap it was shot through the back of the head.

Travelling together, we were lucky to get a cabin for the two of us. So little travelling in ships is done now that I do not know if bunks are still allotted to total strangers, so long as they are of the same sex. It always seemed odd, when no one would dream of doing this in a hotel. On board it was taken for granted and only after a tremendous row in front of the skipper could you get out of the cabin allotted to you. Cicely found this out years later, when, travelling with her three year old daughter, she had a violent alcoholic as her companion for the month's voyage. Also the second-class section of the four berth cabins were six feet square with no porthole. Thirty years later in a Dutch ship, I was staggered to find a cabin for two had plenty of chairs, cupboards and shower and WC of its own.

During the years to come we did quite a bit of travelling between East Africa and England, experimenting with some of the lines then using those seas. We found the Union Castle ships in those days very formal. Carrying the Royal Mail and colonial officials put them in the top drawer. The food was good and strictly British; if apples ran out then we did without dessert, though the ship might call at ports where tropical fruit was plentiful. It is to be hoped that they have changed their ways. The British India line on the other hand, smelt richly of curry, the Lascar crew making us feel we were memsahibs.

On this first voyage our first port of call was Marseilles and then we made for Port Said, coming in at dawn past the long breakwater where the statue of de Lesseps stood. Once tied up we charged ashore to Simon Arts, that shop jam-packed with eastern brass from Birmingham, and Arab robes in artificial silk from Italy, not to mention excruciatingly ugly tapestries depicting camels and pyramids done in shades of fish-paste and coming from I know not where. There were also locally made rough cotton squares with ancient Egyptian figures and motifs appliqued in cotton cloth on them, very gay and costing only a shilling or so apiece. We bought them along with our topees and terai hats. Wherever we went we were jostled by shoe cleaners and the sellers of Turkish delight ('veree good for stomach in the morning'). In order to charm us they called us Mrs Langtry, and if rebuffed called us Mrs McGregor. On board, the Gully Gully man conjured with thin exhausted little chickens, while the fortune tellers showed great insight into human weakness by saying, "My, you have suffered greatly, but you have a brave face," guaranteed to make almost anyone purr.

On returning to the quay we found our ship had moved across to the coaling station. Two gangplanks led to the shore and an endless succession of black figures, men and women, passed up and down with baskets in a thick haze of black dust. This meant that we must take rowing boats to get a-board. We had an alarming trip as the oarsmen bumped, yelled oaths and bashed each other in order to arrive first. Elderly red-faced Sahibs shouted and tried to restore order by whacking their own Arabs with their walking sticks, which seemed to encourage them to fight more vigorously, whilst the Memsahibs cried, "Don't, dear." Nobody capsized and, very hot and dusty, we got up the gangway.

There is a story that in the days before the Suez Canal was dug and opened, people took the short overland route, travelling by train from Port Said to Suez, where they boarded another ship. Half way on this journey the train would stop for dinner at a station restaurant. The meal, always a long time coming, started with exceedingly hot and peppery soup. Whilst the passengers struggled with this, whistles began to blow, flags waved and urgent shouts ordered them aboard the train or else they would be stranded. At last there came a time when an army officer (I hope he was made a Field-Marshall) rebelled. He pointed out very firmly that no ship would sail without so large a number of passengers, so the blasted train could wait and the dinner continue. It was then the highly profitable racket was exposed. There was no dinner. The trick had worked successfully for years and years. I do not know what happened after that, and suspect that the local fowls had their necks wrung and that there was some very quick grilling.

For us now our ship was to start after dark, a searchlight in the bow, moving down the Canal to tie up to allow home-going ships to pass. Ships from which voices called: "You're going the wrong way!" When dawn came, we were in a strange new world of still blue water with the barren wastes of Sinai and the hills of Africa rose pink in the morning light.

Now we must accustom ourselves to a week in the Red Sea, praying for a head wind to keep us cool. On later trips we were to have a stern wind so that stokers and cooks collapsed and the ship was turned round to get fresh air blowing through her. Then the captain allowed the second-class passengers who used the well deck to come onto the main deck where there was a faint breeze, whereat some first class passengers objected. It was the same snobbery as that found in one of the Nairobi clubs, where a young man, if a farmer or cadet government officer, could become a member, whilst his elder brother, who was a Regimental Sergeant Major (RSM), was barred.

After three days we put in at Port Sudan where the railway ran up to Khartoum. Our ship was loaded with rolling stock and lines; great heavy things came out of the hold with only a few inches clearance and if dropped would surely go straight through the bottom. The cranes were manned by real Fuzzie-Wuzzies, splendid lithe people with huge pompoms of hair, checked loincloths and curly daggers. They walked like proud warriors and handled their great machines with skill. There were merchants here selling ivory beads and carvings, also an extremely grubby ancient who brought from out of his rags a small piece of filthy cloth in which were pearls.

Whether it was the time of the year or because there was a storm brewing, the whole inlet was packed with fish. They lay fin to fin alongside the ship, grey, red, green and black. When we hired a boat to row us across to a bay where we could bathe, the fish leaped out of the water as the oars went in, and when we swam, myriads of tiny jewelled bright little ones flipped between our hands.

As soon as we left the inlet the temperature dropped twenty degrees or more and the rest of the Red Sea was grey and stormy until we were into the Indian Ocean and reached Aden.

Many British have come and gone that way and are now gone for good. Back to the beloved small lush fields, the modest seaside hotel, or out to the strange new life and death of the East, with responsibility heavy on their shoulders. This was where the world of Kipling starts. Dust, smell, the slender sinister dark men with their bubbling camels. Down by the sea front was the Club; on the veranda the long chairs and unpolished tables, and, inside, most strangely, I thought, large framed prints of kittens tumbling out of baskets. Were they there to remind the Empire Builders that Nanny at the Rectory was just like Britannia? Hovering over them, ready to say, "Now then Master John, we can't have that. Eat your bread and butter before cake!"

A week after Aden through navy blue seas white with foam and gay with flying fish, we were making landfall at Mombasa. Nothing remarkable about the coastline, just low bush-covered hills. At last we could see the Island, its white buildings, palms and mango trees, and were slipping into Kilindini, the deep water harbour. Then David Flett rushed on board and grabbed his Helen, to tear off to the DO's office in order to get married before noon, it being Saturday. We in our wedding finery were left to sort the luggage and get it on the train, due to leave at 4.30. A tedious business this, in a huge iron shed. The boxes were dumped on the quay and someone who knew the alphabet called out the first letter on the label. The box went on to someone else's head, who chanted the letter, but as he went probably changed it from B to G or T, so they were stacked in a jumble. We got most of it sorted out, but had to leave the key of our precious chest of drawers with a large smiling gentleman, known as Diamond Juma, with instructions to get it through customs and sent up country. It was a pity the key was lost so that it arrived many weeks later with the front wrenched open, and fastened again by nailing a piece of wood across, into the mahogany chest inside. It was a great joy to come across it more than fifty years later in a cousin's house, with its scars obliterated after years of polishing.

The train got off not long before nightfall, crossing the bridge and starting the long haul up the thickly wooded hill, stopping frequently at small stations where there seemed to be no platform to speak of, but large crowds of people who had come to what was the social event of the day. The Kenya and Uganda Railway has had many books written about it, none better than *The Lunatic Express*. Why express I cannot imagine, as it never got up any speed, stopping frequently at irregular places. Perhaps it was lunacy to build it as it brought many problems still to be solved, though the intention was good. Maybe the author thought it had to take on so daunting a task, which would cost and change so many lives. In 1922 it ran from Mombasa to Kisumu on Lake Victoria, where small steamers linked it up to ports in Uganda and Tanganyika. Short branches ran down to the soda lake at Magadi and out to a coffee-growing district near Nairobi. The most stupendous bit of engineering was getting it down onto the floor of the Rift Valley and out again, climbing some 2,000 feet or more. In the early days coaches and wagons were lowered down by cable to be linked to another engine waiting below. By the time we arrived a not so permanent way ran down the side of the valley. Burning firewood, the engine stopped to load up and take on water. The carriage windows were fitted with wire gauze as well as wooden slats, all helping to keep out the largish chunks of red-hot charcoal.

Also, as the sleepers were laid on the bare earth, a cloud of ochre-red dust billowed in, and up through the floor boards. We were warned to tie up our heads in scarves and plaster ourselves with cold cream, as by morning we should look like Red Indians. I think the carriages were old Indian stock; the richest and nicest were those which had two compartments with a wash place between them and small verandas at the ends. The train stopped at stations for meals (they did not play the Suez game), and while we dined stewards put out bedding rolls on the seats. It was all very leisurely, and if you were nimble you could climb onto the roof and admire the view. Later we became used to the up-country habit of catching a goods train and arranging with the engine driver to unlock a truck, where we could sit on our bedding roll very comfortably. He would stop the train for a meal and it did not seem to matter if we held up traffic, as we dawdled along this way on the single-track line. We did not think this selfish behaviour, having adapted ourselves to a timeless place where travel was crazy, and anything might happen.

So, well greased and with all the shutters up, we spent the night, and as first light peered out, we found out we were out of the bush. An immense stretch of country rolled for miles, tawny and dappled as a lion's skin, until volcanic mountains reared up, range upon range, angular and blue. The air was limpid and cool, so clear that surely you could slip your fingers round the sedate little clouds that hung in the sky. Oh Lord, what a morning! Gold grass, slashed with black where fire had passed, scarlet ant heaps, angular little thorn trees. It was as bright and gay as a child's picture book. And then the animals. At seventy plus you hold your tongue and do not say, "Ah, but you never saw the old Africa!" When the young take you to the game parks or show you their slides, you admire and rejoice that the wild life is being treasured. Then it was like the great Serengeti migration of wildebeest going on all over the place. Grunting, they cavorted in elaborate arabesques, and along with them were uncountable numbers of dun-coloured oryx, eland moving in close formation at a smooth trot, hartebeest with their droll faces, looking rather badly constructed until they leaped into a gallop. Amongst them fat zebra bickering, yapping like small dogs all mixed up with the fox-coloured Grant's and Thomson's gazelles, with here and there ostrich and the dignified secretary birds. Then floating along with their soft eyes looking gently on all things, the giraffe ranging in colour from lemon yellow to burnt orange.

Very close at hand a ridiculous thing was going on. At the centre of a newly cropped ring of grass was a tussock. On it perched the velvet black King of Seven, Widow Bird, not much larger than a sparrow but with a tail of black feathers any cock would he proud to own. Here he performed his ritual mating dance, flinging himself into the air and toppling back to his perch again, while his demure, grey wives sat round and admired him. By this time we were travelling down to the Athi River, the last lap to Nairobi. The plain to the right of the line became empty of game, while they still crowded the area to the left. The animals already knew that this side was reserved for them. The other was dangerously near the town and was open to anyone with a licence to shoot. Even so, we soon learnt that leopards would come into the suburbs looking for dogs, considered by them to be a delicacy, and all over the town at night you heard the noise of hyenas overturning rubbish bins, and quarrelling over the contents.

It was true that we looked like Red Indians and had to do a great deal of scraping before trying to wash the dust off and make ourselves presentable for arrival at the one platform station. Built of stone, it was quite a superior building and fairly seething with Indians, Somalis, Africans and Europeans.

Outside lay the wide avenue of Government Road, first the railway-houses built of corrugated iron and then the town. The majority of the shops were of iron and sported verandas across the side-walk, though there were a few stone buildings. At the further end of Government Road stood the Norfolk Hotel with trees in front where Roosevelt and that great hunter, Selous, had tethered their horses. It was presided over by a good looking, white-haired woman in a stiff-collared white blouse and long black skirt, known to everyone as Auntie, and, it was said, hailing from Texas.

The other wide street ran at right angles up to where the half-finished cathedral stood. Here was the newly opened New Stanley Hotel, a couple of banks, a cinema, a railway office built to look like a railway engine and the one-storied District Commissioner's office. Both streets were very wide so that a wagon and eight span of oxen could turn in them. Scattered about behind was the Indian Bazaar smelling richly of spice and other things - well, there was no modern plumbing even in the New Stanley.

Nowadays Nairobi is a swarming city of great office buildings, hotels, noble and peculiar towers and Government offices, a bewildering place stretching far and wide. It has been blessed in having had a genius who planted avenues of flowering trees, and trained bougainvilleas of every colour to make carpets and festoons, while the centre of the roundabouts look as if they had existed from prehistoric times, with their great boulders and strange cacti. In 1922 the town would have made a good set for a Western. Bounded by the wooden Ainsworth Bridge and a district called Parklands there was a big tree, its polished bole used by elephants as a scratching post, and beyond the Cathedral was the Hill where lay the hospital, the houses of the Government officials and the Club. This last, as it is now, should be preserved, complete with members, under a glass case.

These two main streets were busy, or so we thought then, with motors, many of them T-Fords, mule gharis and rickshaws. A deep concrete open drain separated road from the pavement. A year or two later we made friends with a man who would call in at the farm. He was a Swedish blacksmith named Nielson, who had come to Africa via

New Zealand. A short man with tremendous shoulders and arms, he sported a long fair moustache, Viking style, nearly touching his chest and had a flattened nose. He was often drunk and had a tendency to spit on the floor, drunk or sober. His manners were beautiful and he never swore before ladies. He told how, when rather more drunk than usual, he had taken on the Nairobi police force. Having got his back to a wall and with one of those open drains before him he had only to wait until an askari dropped his eyes to step across it to knock him out. According to him the drain was quite full of askaris when the Irish police officer arrived. "Ah, that's a grand fight you're having," says he, "and I think now we'll just be getting along to the station." Nielson agreed but said firmly that he would go like a gentleman. This he did, travelling alone in a rickshaw with the police officer following in another. He really was a very nice man. When Eric asked him how he came by his flat nose he explained he had shared a tent with a friend. He was sleeping soundly when the friend awoke to see a pink rat sitting on Nielson's face and promptly flattened it and the nose, with a convenient bottle. This woke Nielson up, but there were no hard feelings.

Nowadays when thousands of Europeans come to Kenya on package tours it is very entertaining for us old folk to sit sipping coffee at the Thorn Tree studying Human Life, just as they have come to see the wild life. Small mini-buses painted with zebra stripes draw up and they are pushed into them, armed to the teeth with cameras and all that equipment that goes with photography these days, as well as books on the flora and fauna. They sport the most splendid safari outfits, or heraldic T-shirts, dark glasses, weird hats and blue-rinsed hair. Now and then you spot a really fine specimen of a stringy old-timer in a battered old car with an equally ancient African retainer, a reminder of the time when, if you saw a new face at the hotel you sat up saying, "Now who on earth can that be?" There are no more memsahibs down shopping from the Hill, wearing white topee and tussore suits, and their smart rickshaws pulled by one 'boy' and pushed by another, in a livery of white jumper and shorts trimmed with a coloured braid.

Some people say that on arrival all Africans look alike. This may be true in other parts of the continent, but surely not here. There are 44 tribes and many of them are as different in physique as a Norwegian to a Greek, especially in the days before they took to European dress. One prudish mission had dressed their women converts in hideous sponge-bag check dresses. The long skirt gathered into a high yoke above their large breasts, the mop cap of the same stuff on their small elegant heads, made them look positively obscene, and it was said that this costume was so coveted that women would go to any lengths to get it. How much more seemly and splendid was their own traditional way of dress. Their well-greased bronze skin, the supple dark leather robe, great clusters of coloured beads at the temples, copper and iron wire covering arms, legs and neck. Heavy and uncomfortable maybe, but they did not seem aware of it. Both men and women of several tribes loaded their ears with plugs of wood until in old age the lobes touched their shoulders.

The Swahili and Somali women wore brilliant cotton clothes swathed round their bodies and over their heads, while the menfolk wore the smart embroidered skull cap and the ankle-length Kanzu.

Spears had to be left behind when the young warriors wished to see the wonders of the town; there were plenty of them painted with red ochre, their hair twisted into hundreds of cords after the fashion of ancient Egypt. The Maasai were seldom seen, having little interest in Western follies, lithe and supercilious, they silently mocked us in our elaborate clothes and clumping boots. Then the Somalis, robed, turbaned and swathed in scarlet or emerald shawls, their minds on the Prophet and their elaborate business concerning the herds they had brought with them from the north.

There had been trade between India and the coast of East Africa for no-one knows how many centuries. Then other Indians came to build the railway, and with them came the little iron sheds where they set up shop, brought their families over and prospered. Now they were a very large community trading, banking and working on the railway, so adding to the pageant of colour and styles in every kind of costume from gold embroidered saris to the humble man in his dhoti.

We discovered that the women of the open plains carry their loads

72

on their heads. Those of the hills carry loads on their backs supported by a strap round the forehead, bent almost double. Our reaction was of horror that they should be so burdened. Later we came to learn that it is the woman who cultivated land and carried loads, whilst the man carried the spears to defend her. Also it was not appreciated if one sympathised with her lot. She was immensely proud, as an old woman, to be able to hump large sacks of potatoes up and down steep hills, or travel for miles to return with so large a load of firewood, just the only bit of her to be seen were her feet.

After a few days absorbing the sights and sounds of Nairobi and doing last-minute shopping, we were on board the train again, winding through Kikuyu country and down into the Rift Valley until we came to Gilgil. Here we left the train in the middle of the night. It was a very small place then, all the buildings save one, being of corrugated iron. One was interesting, being a warning not to take orders literally. It was a two-roomed house and had stood in the township of Nakuru. The owner wished it moved and instructed a builder to take it to pieces and rebuild it on the plot he had bought in Gilgil. On being asked how he wanted it sited he said, vaguely, that it should be square with the plot. Since the plot was diamond shaped, the conscientious man cut every piece of iron and floor board to construct a diamond shaped bungalow. It wasn't too bad from the outside, but when you went indoors you began to think you had come over queer, or perhaps needed glasses, as corners rushed towards you or ran away.

The one brick building was a small hotel, planned very like a country railway station and owned by a titled lady who was French, and exactly like the one who was so kind to Barbar the Elephant. Managing the place was a hearty, rural couple. The husband nearly killed himself when he put two of those gas bullets you fix in a wire meshed syphon to make soda water. It exploded with the noise of a bomb, sending chunks of glass and metal past their heads. Great was the occasion if you arrived after a pig had been killed. You feasted on every kind of pork-based dish and were thankful for the delicious food, more so if you knew you had 68 miles to travel to the farm in which to walk it off. Coming down from the farm we found we could not sleep on the first night in a brick building, being unused to the stuffiness of a room with a ceiling and glassed windows. We would then go down with a streaming cold as we had no resistance to germs.

In Gilgil we waited for the wagon to arrive. Somehow Eric had arranged for it to come on a certain date, given a day or two either side. Getting messages to people was difficult. The quickest way was to send a runner — yes the real cleft stick was used, as he did not have a pocket – and the sight of the letter gave him a right of way across other people's farms. You could send a telegram or letter. That meant they went into the post office pigeon hole to wait until the recipient called for it. This might not be for weeks.

Anyway, our wagon turned up after a couple of days - a splendid twelve-foot-long affair, built on the same plan as those of the Voertrekkers, and covered by a hood made of bent saplings and a tarpaulin.

The crew, if that is the right word, was made up of M'baraiki, a youth who walked behind, whose job it was to turn the iron handle which put the brakes on. He never could remember which way it turned. This was held against him. Not by me, as being ambidextrous I never knew myself. The second youth was called Ashika Kamba, which being translated means rope holder. He led the first pair of oxen by a rawhide thong attached to their horns, round any craters,

*Cicely and Eric by the ox wagon at Shalcross's Camp,
about 22 miles from Gilgil.*

boulders or tree trunks. Oxen being oblivious to such things, though willing to pull until they collapse, once the wagon is really stuck. The captain of the crew was N'Dereva himself, who wore a long greatcoat and a battered felt hat, trimmed lavishly with ostrich feathers. The badge of his calling was a huge whip, its stock six foot high and its thong long enough to touch the furthest span of oxen. An expert is able to flick a fly off a beast's ear, and the whip was not used for beating the animals, but to encourage them and advertise the arrival of the wagon by being cracked. It requires great strength to do this and the noise can be heard for miles. Coming down from the farm it was loaded with hides and tins of ghee and even maize, if there had been a good crop, and N'Dereva would have a list made by neighbours who needed spare parts, tools, medicine or anything else not to be had in the local store.

Before going on I must apologise for breaking into various words which are not English. They are part of the history of East Africa. Swahili as spoken on the coast is a complex difficult language, part Arabic, part Bantu, with a few Indian and Portuguese words, and now plenty of English words Africanised, such as Manawari for a naval ship. Up country Swahili is a grammar-free pidgin language and the inter-tribal speech. Africans seem to prefer a vowel between consonants, and they generally prefix the word with N' or M' and Wa for the plural. When after the Boer War many South Africans trekked up to Kenya they brought their words for the landscape; drift for a ford, and so on. To make things complicated every European had a nickname which you had to memorise. This was easy as they fitted. Anyone a bit of a dandy would be Bwana Maridadi, while someone who was corpulent, would be called Bwana Tumbo. One small dark man was Bwana Dudu – insect. He found this trying, pointing out that he was a great hunter, so why not call him Bwana Simba, the lion. "But you look like an insect," was the reply. We always hoped that Mbuzi was the nearest in pronunciation to our last name Booth, rather than meaning we looked like a goat.

At Gilgil on that first journey, we loaded up and N'Dereva called to the grazing cattle, which came two by two and lowered their heads meekly for their yokes. Then the whip cracked, their names were called, the young boy picked up the thong and the great cart rolled forwards at a steady two-and-a-half miles an hour. Like a ship it heaved and rolled over the earth track. Every now and again there would be a large hole where an ant bear, mistaking the red earth for a termite hill, had burrowed a small deep crater, quite deep enough to destroy the springs of a car, but not the wagon, as it had none. For the first 14 miles the road wound in and out of a series of valleys amongst thick shrubs. Then, before sunset, we were out of the last onto a wide shallow plain stretching away to the Aberdare Mountains.

Here the cattle were outspanned and allowed to feed until it was dark and a good fire was blazing! The fire would be kept going all night, while the men and boys slept in the warmth and the oxen huddled round, knowing they were safe in its light. Supper was cooked and we were soon in our blankets, Cicely and I under the hood on a load of sacks of rice. Eric chose to lie underneath, and though colder, the hard earth was flatter than those sacks. We were now 6,000 feet up and the air was chill with the stars blazing down, Orion directly overhead and the Southern Cross low in the heavens. There was the smell of crushed grass, wood smoke and the sweet breath of the cattle, the low murmur of talk and the heart-jerking scream of the tree-hyrax, three descending notes and a series of grunts.

At 5 am when it was still black night, a hand came through the tarpaulin with tin mugs of scalding tea, lovely to sip as we wriggled into the few bits of clothing we had taken off. Then we rolled up our blankets and climbed down for breakfast as the dawn began to break. The cattle were grazing, but as soon as the sun was up we were off again.

A few months later we took six hours to get the wagon up that last hill. The thick cement-like mud and ruts were so deep that the great cart was in danger of turning over, and had to be unloaded twice during our two-mile struggle. Our present journey was during the dry months and we were lucky to have no setbacks. Close on the left lay the hills covered with forest, some of the cedar trees advancing through the laurel-like bush down to the road. Great trees which belong to the

Shall we get there tonight?

juniper family, they were swathed in long scarves of grey lichen. Some had been burnt by honey-hunting N'dorobo, those sly forest people much harried in the past by stronger tribes. One of these trees stood close by the track and as the wagon passed by we realised the bole was a hollow shell through which we could see daylight. The mild breeze caused it to twist and creak and we held our breath, hoping the rumbling wheels would not bring it down.

Every few miles we bumped across little bridges over streams that ran to join the Narok River, the road more or less on the route the railway would take some years later, and where a couple of small townships would spring up.

Our daily pattern was ruled by the sun and the ox. We would rumble along until the sun was nearly overhead and the only shadow immediately under the wagon. There we would sit for two hours or so for the cattle to feed and ourselves too. One of the Africans would start a fire, lit by a piece of wood he had picked out of the one we had extinguished on starting in the early morning. Somehow by waving it about and occasionally blowing upon it he had kept it smoldering, a skill we have lost. There would soon be tea and bully beef and biscuits and large lumps of stodgy cold maize meal porridge to be eaten. By 2 pm we would set out again, stopping before sunset for the beasts to graze, and men to gather firewood for the protecting fire. "Never go out of the firelight without a hurricane lamp," was a rule we found embarrassing when the call of nature sent us looking for cover in the treeless plain. The cattle were quick to hear any alarming noises and would draw in closer for safety and our sleeplessness was not all due to hard sacks and altitude. The nights could be really cold and sometimes a fine drizzle would fall. Strangely enough, the wagon's crew would then wrap their heads up in their blankets and sleep soundly in this self-made fug.

By the third night we were 8,000 feet up and crossed the Equator a mile or so before reaching Thomson's Falls, now called Nyahururu, meaning waterfall. There is a two-hundred foot gorge where the Narok River plunges without a break. In 1922 there was the wooden bridge and a couple of thatched huts for use of the police or forestry people. It was cold as soon as the sun was down, and we were glad to find the forestry officer camped there with a huge bonfire built with the lavishness of people who have forests bigger than most English counties from which to gather their kindling. He was a school friend of my brother's, so they yarned away whilst we toasted ourselves. This district was packed with rhino, elephant and buffalo, the three most dangerous animals to meet in dense bush, but he said he was safer when he did not carry a gun. Then he had no instinctive reaction to defend himself, and stood quietly waiting for the creatures to move off, which they invariably did.

It was here that we left the Rumuruti road, turning over the bridge and away to the right where the track ran through a difficult stretch. In this high damp country the soil was a stiff paste, while the rain washed the ruts into deep trenches where even the big wagons could become hopelessly stuck or overturn. Should this calamity happen the only thing to do was to walk to the nearest farm and borrow another team of oxen. It could happen that the number of straining animals could pull the front axle off. Then there was nothing for it but to find a Seychellois or Goan wagonwright to make repairs, and he might live many miles away. So the navigation of Red Banks, as it was called, was always a matter of anxiety. Some twenty years later both Eric and Cicely farmed at this spot and now the huge forest is cut down and the district thickly populated by small-holders.

Once through the forest the land fell away and before us lay Laikipia. Sixty miles away or more stood Mount Kenya, the great crags and glaciers dazzling in the morning light, until clouds swathed them from sight. Yet in this tawny undulating country was the lemon-green Pesi swamp, where our new home was to be. The oxen began to step out. They had not cared for the rank grazing of the high country and could smell the warm ripeness of the lowland grass.

Every now and again wheel tracks would break away from the main track to where our neighbours were making their farms and soon we called in on a couple whose house was close by the road. This homestead was our first introduction to what lay at hand. Thatched whitewashed cottages, very like the ones in the Fylde district at home, were set on three sides of a square buried in geraniums and carnations. The center cottage was the living room, the floor was hard-packed

Eric, Cicely and Joan Booth with Kamau travelling by oxcart.

earth and there was a fireplace. The carved over mantel and the beams were blackened with wood smoke and you looked up into the thatched roof. It seemed as if the place had stood for centuries, and we were given a warm welcome, partly, we hoped, for ourselves, but also as bearers of news from Nairobi and Britain.

By the afternoon when the clouds began to clear from the mountain to show it golden and rose, we emerged from the thorn bush into open grassland. N'Dereva began to whistle and crack his great whip. The roofs and bomas showed up and the farm hands turned out to welcome us. "Jambo," they cried and we replied, "Jambo! Habari? What news?"

"Mzuri," was always the reply; it means "Good," and was followed with "lakini" which is the portentous "But." Then followed the list of disasters which the reporter told with relish, how the lions have killed so many cattle or horses died from fever, or possibly the loss of grazing from bush fires, ending with something comforting such as that the hens were laying. Like all people living on the brink of death and hunger, the African has a tremendous armoury of humour. Disaster has to be comic or you can't endure it, so they relish retelling the awful events, with gestures and hoots of laughter. It's akin to the songs soldiers sing in warfare, or the splendidly funny "Ain't it grand to be bloomin' well dead" that describes a grand funeral during the great depression.

This time the "lakini" was that the house had not had any thing further done to it since Eric had left, being just a thatched roof held up by poles, with some scantling where the floor should be. The choice was whether we slept out of doors with the possibility of being eaten by lions or hyenas, or the certainty of being devoured more slowly by fleas in the little square hut, Eric's old home. Whilst he was in England, it had been used by the poultry. One step inside and your legs looked as if they had been sprinkled lavishly with black pepper – pepper, which enjoyed our delicious European blood. After the first night I counted over eighty bites on one leg, the rest of me being just as well bitten. Also hens are single-minded birds, and they had chosen a corner of the hut to lay their egg. The moment the door was opened

80

a crack a feathered bomb hit you and with hysterical squawks fought its way in and then darted to its corner and laid your breakfast egg.

To make things more like a cabin in the bog, it rained copiously, and the thatch leaked, a grand incentive to start building, and that we did. Cedar wood from the East African pencil cedar splits easily, so every nail hole must be drilled before the slabs were fixed to the framework. There was no glass for the windows and we hoped chicken wire would keep the larger animals out. It did, but not the insects. They flew in swarms when fires were lit, not that they bit, but for the most part they were large, bumping and flopping about in an irritating way. Also, though termites don't eat cedar, they do like the bark and could travel up to settle happily in the thatch, occasionally letting go and landing on one or into one's teacup.

The wood for building came in the usual timeless African way, resulting in long delays. We developed great skill at stepping from one joist to another. When the floor-boards did arrive, we devised a rather

Eric in front of the third hut he had built on farm 730 in Rumuruti.

tiring technique for laying them. They had warped badly so the only way to get them nailed in place was for Cicely and me to sit bracing our feet against the plank, shove it against the one already laid down, begging Eric to be quick with his hammer before cramp set in.

The large cracks between the slabs making the walls were covered with folded newspaper - the termites enjoyed this. Over this were fixed mats of dried papyrus some six feet high, a delightful yellow and green colour smelling sweetly of hay. On them went the applique mats we had bought at Port Said. For curtains we put up some heavy silk with art nouveau designs, discarded long ago in England, and brought merely as packing. Wired through top and bottom post, they kept the wind out. We already had a table Erie had made and some bentwood and cowhide chairs. To these were added the furniture bought in Nairobi, dressed up in the gay cotton we had with us. There were some shelves for books, making it a very pleasant room. It had no door, why I cannot remember, unless the wood had run out. This did not worry us except when a couple called with a pack of thirteen large dogs. Well fed on zebra meat, smelling horribly, covered with fleas and dust, they were persistently affectionate.

In our two little bedrooms we had our camp beds and packing cases. Those holding two four-gallon petrol tins were easy to come by.

'Barton' Rumuruti Built 1922.
Laikipia

Joan and Cicely helped Eric build the main house at Rumuruti in 1922.

Joan in front of the main house, named Barton after the family home in England. The house faced toward the Aberdares.

It was interesting to find how many different pieces of furniture could be made by joining them together. Given some legs and a coat or two of paint they looked well, especially when I found some oil paint used for farm machinery and could spend a happy time evolving gay Scandinavian-looking flowers on the panels.

For a spare room a round hut went up wonderfully quickly once the central pole was set up and tamped home firmly. It was good to see what a communal thing building was. The men did the thatching and wove the wattle for the walls, whilst the women trampled the mud and cow-dung in a nearby pit, until it was of the right stiffness to daub on the walls. All this was accompanied with singing and story telling. Stories surely, that from the tone of voice, now squeaky, now growly, were about the little wise one, Kalulu the hare, the ancestor of Brer Rabbit, whose cunning always vanquishes the big animals.

The daub, once dry, was white washed with wood ash. The door was higher than those of the African huts. Cool by day, warm by night, the new house was ideal for Africa. Somehow you knew in your bones that your forefathers had built like this, so it satisfied something at the bottom of your mind. This is the place of women, the homemakers. Every member of the family has an appointed place, from father, the defender and hunter, to the latest new-born baby and chicken, which nestles in safety and warmth with its human companions.

Our water had to be brought up from the swamp half a mile away, in four-gallon *debes* carried on men's heads. Then it was tipped into a galvanised iron tank. Under this a fire was lit in the evening. For drinking it had to be well boiled, then filtered, Even so it was rather thick and greenish. Later my eldest brother came out on holiday with his wife and she kindly brought us gifts of bath salts. Soon we noticed a fragrance pervading everything, including the butter. We discovered that hauling extra water was thought to be too much of an effort, so that baths were being returned to the boiler. My sister-in-law never took to life upcountry after that.

We planted two pepper trees by the house and grew geraniums, using the bath water for these, but they were a poor lot. We tried to make a garden down by the swamp, but it came to nothing under the feet of a huge mother hippo and her young. My old fear of making the journey to the walled garden when a little girl came back, as I walked that half-mile, imagining a rhino or leopard in every bush. Of course, a well used path would be a most unlikely place for game to linger, but that did not stop my qualms. I still prefer to see big game from the veranda of a game park hotel.

It was desperation that made us try to grow vegetables. A wild spinach growing on old boma sites kept us from scurvy, otherwise there was nothing fresh. Potatoes could be bought in the township and an elderly man would walk the fifty miles from Nyeri with a large gourd full of delicious green bananas. He sold them to us at a shilling a hundred. Another man came with eggs, but these had to be tested. Those which floated in a bowl of water were discarded. This did not upset the seller, who at the end of the deal returned the rejected eggs to the gourd and went on his way in the hope of meeting somebody less guileful, or who likes them bad.

We took joyfully to the upcountry custom of having our sundowners, then our baths, eating our dinner in pyjamas and dressing gowns. This was very much the custom, some people making a point of having really beautiful dressing gowns for occasions when friends were staying. Evening clothes were for dances or Nairobi. The only occasion of dressing for dinner in the bush that I know of was when the Governor was making one of his safaris to visit the District Commissioners of the Colony. When in the Northern Frontier he met up with one who was known to be so enamoured of desert life that he wore Somali costume - a checked cloth round the waist kept in place by belt and dagger and sandals. He read him a lesson, saying he was letting the side down by going native. At dinner His Excellency turned up in his dressing gown, while the DC came in white tie, tails and decorations.

Our neighbours, who lived a mile or so away, had a tennis court made from the brick-hard murram crushed and well rolled, making a good hard court. In the other direction the Fletts had settled into their house some two miles off, so we had plenty of company. Across the swamp lived a lively Australian and his mother, as well as a Boer family, one of the many who had trekked up from South Africa at the end of the war in 1902. They shot their meat and grew some mealies. The young people were practically illiterate as it was some years before they acquired schools. Their houses were built in the style of their forefathers, mud and wattle with hard polished floors, made by mixing ox blood with clay and dung. On Sundays the men got into uncomfortable black suits, the womenfolk into purple velvet dresses and steel beads. When you called, they sat solemnly round the room and made stilted conversation about crops and the weight of their womenfolk, a source of much pride. "Ja, my wife is well; she

Eric, Cicely and Joan with neighbours in Rumuruti in January 1923, looking at the Christmas numbers that had recently arrived.

weighs sixteen stone. My daughter weighs seventeen stone!" Chat was very hard going, especially if an older woman sat there silent, because, having seen her home burnt and endured the concentration camps, she had vowed never to speak English. Their young men were trading their wagons for lorries and with the money they made running transport during the war, they began to set up businesses and buy land. They planted vast acres of maize and wheat, enough to feed Kenya and export as well. Large Protestant churches, houses and schools were built. Then in the 1960s independence came and they returned south. Their farms were, for the most part, cut up into smallholdings.

Our African cook could make a good stew or roast a joint in a *debe* thrust into the hot ashes of his wood fire. Somehow he could adjust the heat to bake cakes and bread. This last was made with a strange brew of yeast – a bit of last week's dough, water, sugar and a few raisins in a bottle. Every so often a loud bang told us that the yeast had exploded. Then cook would have to visit our neighbours and start a fresh brew. Should we need a small amount of butter it was made by rubbing a stick with a piece of buck's vertebrae at the end between the palms of the hands to swizzle the cream round. For large amounts we bought an end-over-end churn. When made, it was rendered down on the fire until it was clear and then strained into a *debe* and soldered

Joan and Cicely with Mr Crane heading for Gilgil in the 1920s.

down. It was sent to Nairobi and sold to the Indian traders who gave a good price for this unadulterated ghee.

There was also soap to be made. Very course and mottled blue, it was made by refining fat and adding slaked caustic soda and washing blue. The art is to see that the temperatures are exactly equal. Later I read that the early settlers in America made soda by filtering water through wood ash, and I wish we had known then how to make the wooden hopper needed. Hippo fat was considered to be much the best for soap, so Eric shot an enormous one, and was nearly obliterated when 14 of its companions rose out of the long grass and trundled into the papyrus. As the hippo was two miles from the house, he raced back to collect all hands to cut the animal up. By the time he got back with his men, he found that the whole neighbourhood had swarmed to this marvellous supply of meat and there was nothing left but vultures cleaning up the messy bones. At other times Eric kept us supplied with antelope meat; it kept well since it didn't have any fat.

CHAPTER 6

First Year in the Bush

T he first year of our life in the bush was most unusually wet. This provided splendid grass for the cattle, but it began to grow less as the game was driven by lions into the neck of land between the Pesi and Morogo rivers, now too deep for fording. Looking out of the house one morning I counted over 300 zebra on the plain, and these were only a few. At night it was frightening when they stampeded, coming towards the house like a charge of cavalry, and somehow rushing past the huts and not piling up on the veranda. Later when a fence was put up, of stout posts and steel wire, they hurled themselves through it and down the steep rocky slope into the valley. How they did this without leaving a trail of blood and beasts with broken legs is a mystery.

This year the elephants did not make their annual journey from the Aberdares to the Ol Arabal hills to the north. Eric had lost his kitchen roof a year earlier when they came through the farm; no doubt the smoky grass was a pleasant change of diet, rather like kippers, I should think. In fact they gave up coming for many years until Rumuruti had grown to be a sizeable village, but then they stuck to their old route, taking them through the Club and main road. Those of our friends whose land lay next to the forest, saw more of them. One Scottish friend was charged by a beast and only dropped it when it was nearly on top of him, "Did you aim for the head or the heart?" Eric asked him.

"Man, Ah no aimed at the head nor the heart. I just aimed at the Elephant," he answered.

Joan, Cicely and Eric with their wagon in the 1920s.

As all the rivers were in flood, our stores became very depleted. Eggs we had, and milk. Meat was plentiful as there were countless antelope and game birds, but we got down to a couple of pounds of rice, a tin of syrup and two candles before the wagon got through. It was the candles which we valued most. Once finished we would have had to go to bed at 6:30 pm when night fell.

About this time we became more mobile, having bought three mules. Very small they were, but exceedingly tough. A hippo-hide whip made no impression when you tried to urge them out of their jiggling trot, a pace guaranteed to make you saddle-sore in next to no time. One mule had had an encounter with a rhino, so we both had a bad go of nerves when passing a clump of bushes, its ears going up and its pace becoming very mincing. I hung on praying it would not buck. Having no shoulders to speak of and being able to inflate and deflate its belly, it was needful to have a breast band and crupper to keep the saddle in place. Hard to believe, but I swear that Eric's mule bucked and elongated itself in such a way that my poor brother landed some way in front of the animal on the small of his back, with his feet still in the stirrups and the girth unbroken.

The poultry did well, roaming about in their search for ants and

CRUPPER, GIRTH and all.

Eric's mule bucked him off, crupper, girth and all.

grasshoppers. For one half of the year they sat at midday in a row on the north side of the house, for the other, on the south side, where there would be a foot or two of shade. Somehow we came to own a turkey cock. It would parade up and down waiting for one of us to cross over to the privy or one of the huts, whereupon it would hurl itself on its victim, giving a blow from the wing like that of a cricket bat. It never attacked if you fixed your eye on it with a fierce stare.

Much later we had a tragi-comedy with ducks and turkeys. A drake was bought and we looked forward to having dear little ducklings, but the drake had been hatched by a turkey and so thought he was one. All day long he pursued the embarrassed turkeys, while his poor would-be wives waddled after him. He never learned. At the same time I was kept on the run as a brood of chicks thought I was their mother, along with two hefty bottle-fed lambs. These charged into the house after me, like small wooly tanks, if I did not slam the door in their faces.

In the evening the store would be unlocked and the ration of two pounds of maize meal doled out. Very often the men would not bother to bring a bowl, holding out their one garment, a blanket, for you to tip the maize into. This was just as it says in the Bible: "Put into the bosom, pressed down and running over!" Indeed, life was very much like that of the Old Testament. The yearly anxiety whether the rains would break before the cattle starved, and the joy when it came, with that wonderful smell as the first drops hit the parched earth. The difference between stagnant and living water. The herdsman standing in the narrow doorway of the boma, counting his beasts as they squeezed past him, ready to dab Stockholm Tar on a sore before they made for the flat stone or piece of canvas spread with salt. Even the language was the same: "Bado Kidogo," meaning, "Yet a little while," was used much too often. Less frequently we heard the very earnest: "Kweli, kweli, mimi nasema," meaning, "Truly, truly I say to you." Then there was the importance of the lantern being filled with oil.

Every day we had time for gossip and a bit of medicine when the people came up from their smallholdings. Our medicine was crude; indeed it was not appreciated unless we made it strong, so a dash of Worcestershire sauce enhanced its value.

Most of our neighbours had taken up 6,000-acre farms on a peppercorn rent under the Soldier Settler scheme. Some had wives who, finding life was not as it was in Simla, departed. Some had farmed in East Africa before the war. One sturdy old Scot shot five lions one moonlit night. In these days of conservation it sounds dreadful, but what are you to do when they are eating your horse in the back yard,

Eric earmarking sheep in the 1920s.

while the younger members of the pride are happily swatting your hens. "The place was a cloud of feathers," he said.

One of our neighbours was a South African whom the Africans called Tumbo, the only white man who did not get the prefix Bwana. His wife we admired, for a tougher more gentle woman you cannot imagine. We called on her, and took an elegant tea, sitting up very straight, conversing on housekeeping matters. She had, she said, been having trouble with polecats; one had killed a sitting duck, but all was well. She had put the eggs into her bed and after a few days they all had hatched most successfully. We didn't say we thought it a ticklish business, feeling she might not know the expression, and longed to ask if she had stayed in bed all day before the little ducklings popped out of their shells.

Down river lived 'Daddy Ryan,' an Irish schoolmaster who had come up from South Africa. A widower, he had two children, Bill,

Eric with a lion shot at Barton in about 1927.

aged 14, was back from the World Scout Jamboree and had been congratulated by King George V for having shot a lion. His father said he had wounded the beast, which retreated into the swamp. It was Bill's lion so it was up to him to finish it off. As they worked their way through the papyrus, it roared and young Bill turned and bolted. As he passed, his father heard him say, "Oh Hell, I'm running away," whereupon he stopped, came back and killed it.

"That was the proudest moment for me," said Daddy Ryan. "It takes courage to stand when a lion roars in your face, but far more to be able to stop when you have started running, and come back."

Bill became a famous hunter and his little sister became known in the musical life of the country. They had followed their father with their grandfather, and as communications had broken down Bill, then 12, had to get the little party upcountry, joining a group of new settlers and having a rough time when the oxen died on the long trek over the hills. By sheer luck Daddy rode into Rumuruti when the party turned up. When we knew them, Grandfather had returned to the comforts of South Africa. Daddy's house boasted a piano. This gave us all great pleasure. Wyn would stay there for the shooting. "Daddy," he said, "there are three fleas in my tea."

"Ah yes, they like the warmth," said Daddy.

Looking at an old diary, I am amazed to find an event I had quite forgotten. In these days it seems shocking that there was a tremendous upsurge of feeling amongst the white settlers on hearing that the Government were considering selling land to Indians. We thought of the part of Kenya allotted to us as the White Highlands, and the Indians as people who worked on the railway or kept stores, making a lot of money, which they sent back to their homeland. There was serious talk of protest, even armed protest, with the women and children going to the little townships for safety. It must be remembered that people living far from their neighbours, and struggling for existence can chew over matters of importance or irritation until they grow into an obsession. We would often say of somebody else that it was high time he or she went down to sea-level and learnt to relax. Also the protestors were young ex-service men making what they dreamed, and indeed had been promised, would be a home for their children and children's children. They were building in an uninhabited country with African labour, who came from their own reserves in order to make the eight shillings they needed for hut tax. For the most part they cared for and liked their workers, who could adapt themselves to the weird ways of the Europeans. So we thought of them as hewers of wood and drawers of water, looked after them in a patronising way and told what we considered funny stories about their mistakes. We expected them to be happy in their situation and were ultra-sensitive to any suggestion that other races should share our land as equals. Thankfully the affair died down, and we had no foresight of the heartache that lay ahead.

A very small start was made to form a farmers' co-operative, which would develop in a few years into a big dairy business. Its first manifestation was a two-roomed shack, half of it a store which stood on the next farm. It helped to give us a more varied diet and it was a comfort having such things as nails and paraffin and tinned food. The storekeeper was exactly what a beachcomber would look like. Unwashed, he wore rags and sandshoes with his toes protruding. He would wander over to the house in time for a sundowner and, draping himself over the window-sill, would converse on those grisly murders

Eric and his workers dipping sheep at Barton in 1928.

Cicely and Joan painting flowers at Barton in the 1920s.

he had read about in the more lurid newspapers. In his flat voice he told us his wife wrote to him every day, and sometimes sent telegrams, not that he answered them.

After a few months she turned up, a brisk woman whose great glory was an elaborate crochet dress, which had won a substantial prize in a *Daily Mail* competition. Some months before they had been upcountry in Tanganyika when he had gone down with fever. She had him carried on a stretcher many miles to a hospital. When they came to a crocodile-ridden river she plunged in and by jeering at the porters shamed them into bringing him across. This time she took him back to Nairobi and when next we saw him he was taking the gate money on the racecourse, cleaned up and looking fairly fit.

Once Eric had to make a short trip to Nairobi, so Cecily and I stayed with our next-door neighbours. After breakfast we strolled over to see if all was well at our place, and, hearing one of the dogs screaming, started to run and found ourselves in a swarm of angry bees. They were out to kill, flying straight for the eyes, and if there had not been a very smelly bonfire of stable litter they would have done so. As it was, one dog died, and the other recovered after collapsing several times. Seven hens and the cock also died, their heads and combs encrusted with stings. Those who survived I had dosed with a teaspoonful of whiskey! Standing in the smoke we could see eight men coming up from the swamp with loads of papyrus on their heads. They were strolling along in a dreary state quite deaf to our yells, until the bees struck. The loads went down and they raced away at speed. After a while, perhaps because the bees were trying to keep up with the runners, we were able to leave the smoke and we managed to get back to our friends.

The bees had been living in one of the barrel-like hives the Kikuyu place in trees. Sometimes we would be given a present of honey and very good it was, after it had been diluted, heated and strained, the donor having given what he considered to be the best combs, filled with grubs.

Joan Booth in 1925.

During this first visit we had a short holiday, going by train to Kisumu. As usual we took a train from Gilgil about midnight and next morning found us trundling along the flat lands inhabited by the Luo tribe. In those days the women wore a beaded belt with a bushy little tail at the back. The older men wore most magnificent headdresses made from hippo tusks, feathers and porcupine quills, and everybody smoked long metal pipes. At Kisumu we caught the *Clement Hill*, the flat-bottomed steamer that sailed round the northern half of the lake. It had the disconcerting habit of rising up to the waves and coming down again with a noisy slap, jolting everything aboard, but she seemed very luxurious to us, with spring mattresses in her bunks, delicious food and tropical fruit.

Our first port was the little jetty at Jinja, where the Nile flows out of the lake through a narrow gorge. Jinja and later Thomson's Falls are the two golf courses I know where local rules allow a player to lift a golf ball out of a hippo's footmark. The next day we arrived at Entebbe, the port for Kampala, where the *Clement Hill* took on a cargo of cotton that would travel down to Mombasa to be shipped to Lancashire. Here there was a little railway up to the Capital, not the city of office blocks and hotels, but a dreamy leafy place of thatched houses and the ubiquitous Indian stores. Large Ugandan men dressed in snowy kanzus and little caps, bicycled up and down the hilly roads, whilst a large number of them treadled away at sewing machines. Sauntering about, the Ugandan ladies seemed to spend their time looking beautiful. They wore yards and yards of stiff silky material, tight under the armpits and then swathed and gathered into skirts long and full. Their polished brown shoulders shone from these flower-like gowns and they carried themselves proudly. Emerald, primrose, scarlet and purple, they looked superb. A great pity it is that somebody introduced the fashion of a square-necked, puff-sleeved bodice. It does nothing for modesty and breaks the contrast of rich colour and bronze shining skin.

Kampala is a city of hills; the Anglican and Catholic cathedrals each stand on their own. The Administration offices are on another, and another was the Royal Hill. Here there was a large compound surrounded by a reed fence with an African round hut of truly immense size in the centre. Our guide entered it on his knees and we gazed at the photographs of the late Kabakas, the throne, leopard skins and the gold spears. Kampala had had its tribal and religious wars, its hideous ceremonies and its martyrs, but now it seemed an earthly paradise. It had an abundance of food and, to our amazement, good roads. This came about when the Government gave cars to the Kings and Paramount Chiefs, who saw to it that they had a comfortable ride.

We went back to the station half an hour before the train was due, only to find it gone. The stationmaster explained that there had been such a large number of passengers, seven in all, that there seemed no point in idling about. This was bad luck for us who had to take a taxi, and sad for him as he missed the excitement of having had ten people in his train.

CHAPTER 7

Cicely Meets Jack McDonogh

Shortly after this Cicely and I returned to England, first visiting friends on the coast. We booked a cabin in a small British India ship, which cruised round the Indian Ocean. A tubby little ship, she rolled even when in harbour, but she took us to Zanzibar, another earthly paradise. Here the benign old Sultan took his afternoon drive in an open carriage drawn by two white horses, accompanied by running footmen in gorgeous livery, waving scarlet fly-whisks. He wore the usual gold embroidered blue coat over a snowy robe, and a gold turban and salaamed to his smiling subjects. The town had hardly changed at all, the warehouses on the waterfront and the Cathedral being the only recent buildings and they were far from new.

The hotel had been an Arab mansion and also the gaol. It had the usual magnificent carved doorway, the double doors studded with great brass knobs shaped exactly like lemon squeezers. Inside was the courtyard where a ramp led us to the rooms above, none of these more than ten feet across, although very long. This was because the only beams obtainable were of mangrove wood brought by dhows from the Rufiji swamp in Tanganyika. As you lay in bed you looked through Arabian arches into the tops of coconut palms, which kept up an incessant rustle, and saw the stars blazing between the fronds. Should it happen to blow

Eric dosing a chicken by the kitchen at Barton,
while the cook, Ranje, looks on.

as well as rain, which was not often, there were wooden slatted shutters. Our friends lived in a similar house, as I think did the rest of the small European community, and they were ideal buildings for the tropics.

Everywhere one went was the smell of cloves, the main street and quayside being carpeted with them. They came from the plantations by the Bububu railway. This line was seven miles long, the trains being pulled by small square tank engines, which chuffed happily along the only two streets wide enough to take them. Engine and train were covered with people taking a lift and it practically filled the street. We pedestrians had to dive into the nearest doorway to survive. The World War had developed a trade in 'antiques,' although it was still possible to find genuine old Arab trays and even wooden chests decorated with beautiful brass fretwork. There were plenty of Indian craftsman all making identical ebony elephants. When, with joy, we found an individualist who was making rhinos, we bought six.

It was said that a Kamba man from Kenya working for an NGO decided that his fellow villagers at home could carve wood too, and on returning to Kenya he started them off. Their first carvings were of warriors with very large heads, but they soon were making all manner of figures and animals, fat policemen, gentlemen sitting under umbrellas and mothers clasping their children. Then someone gave them large orders for carvings of identical giraffe and antelopes. I find it rather sad that all that originality has gone and they joined the ranks of Zanzibar's elephant carvers.

Zanzibar was such a peaceful place; it was kept in order by a few large policeman. Their only work seemed to be to gently shoo drunken sailors back to their ships. In the harbour there were the dhows on their yearly trading voyage on the steady monsoon wind from Arabia to the Rufiji and back, just as they had been doing for a thousand years. Strange, timeless old ships, their high, carved sterns are believed to be copied from the first Portuguese galleons, which sailed past. They seemed to be sailed in the most haphazard manner, but really with great skill. The captains looked villainous, each with a curved dagger fixed to the centre of his belt; the older men had their fringe beards dyed a vivid orange with henna. Local fishermen prudently kept close inshore when those dhows started back to Arabia.

After a week we made the short crossing to Dar es Salaam, sailing in the *Windsor Castle* on her last voyage. She had been the latest thing in liners at the beginning of the century and still wore her elaborate upholstery and bobbly-edged curtains like the Victorian dowager she was.

Eric branding cattle in Rumuruti in about 1927.

The one hotel in Dar stank to high heaven. We were used to primitive sanitation and pungent smells, but this outdid them by far. As for the food, we chose boiled eggs and such naturally wrapped fruit as bananas, rather than go in for instant food poisoning. Friends had us for lunch and dinner, for which we were truly thankful, though our up-country appetites cried out for nourishment, whilst our languid friends chatted on and on over sun-downers that saw the sun down by a good three hours.

Dar was the centre of administration with old German buildings on the shores of its lovely inland lagoon, where there are many bays and deserted beaches where you can bathe in safety. The town then was centred on a main cross-roads, Government House and other dwellings being dotted about amongst the palms and mango trees. The local prisoners, wearing neat khaki uniforms, their crime and name sewn on the front - a lot doing time for murder - did the work of road sweeping and firewood delivery with a police askari in charge. One day a party came along when the traffic was at its busiest, with bicycles and cars all dashing home for tiffin. Just when their handcart laden with two-foot logs got into this busy crossroads a wheel came off. Logs rolled in all directions, knocking people off their bikes and getting between wheels. High officials swore, lesser souls yelled, the convicts, their warder, and even the traffic cop who stood on a platform under an umbrella, rushed to pick up the logs. One prisoner, however, kept his head. Hopping onto the platform, he sorted out the traffic jam, getting His Excellency, the Judge and all the other VIPs, as well as the lesser creations, on their way.

Our lowly days in this haven of peace were only marred by the fact that we had booked our passage to Marseilles in a Messageries Maritimes ship, the *Admiral Plane*, coming up from Madagascar no one knew quite when. The shipping agent would ring us up telling us to be ready in a couple of hours, only to admit later that it was yet another case of East African 'Bado Kidogo.' When she did arrive she lay some two miles out to sea. We half-dozen passengers and all our luggage were piled into a most minute steam launch. Even in the lagoon the water was only a few inches below the gunwale and lapped over it at times. Fortunately, it was very calm so we got aboard safely. We found her a comfortable elderly ship, where it was good to see the crew dined out on the fore-deck on the same excellent food that the passengers ate. She did have drawbacks; for one thing she carried a cargo of copra, with its slightly sickly smell and accompanying beetles, as well as the strongest essences of exotic scents. Some of these had burst from their containers. Below decks we were nearly stifled in this rich fug. More alarming was that she had been fitted with an early anti-rolling device, which after Mombasa, got out of order. She began to list badly, and from time to time would keel over the other way. At night it was a matter of clinging on lest you rolled out of your bunk, wondering meanwhile just how far she could go before turning turtle.

An ex-naval man on board remarked that the first real sea she shipped would send her to the bottom, but we managed to reach Port Said where repairs were made. I wonder whether she was the first ship to go through the Canal with fiddles on the tables to prevent the crockery sliding off?

Travelling in ships belonging to other nations is most interesting. You not only study the way of the natives, but learn that we British are a stand-offish, slapdash lot, and I am sure as comic or irritating as we find others. And why not? I am all for variety; for one thing we had to learn to shake hands - on meeting on deck, at meals, and even when coming aboard at Djibouti covered with coal dust. (The ship had one

A cattle sale at Rumuruti in 1927.

of her rolling fits when bunkering and on returning from a trip ashore we found the bottom step of the gangway was four feet above us). There were sartorial rules. For men shorts and shirt-sleeves were taboo in the dining saloon, though it was all right for them to turn up for *petit dejeuner* in pyjamas. As for us Englishwomen, we would get on deck as early as possible and so were damp and crumpled when the others, who had been scurrying about below, very *en deshabille* and waving curling tongs, arrived about eleven o'clock dressed up to the nines and strolled round the deck, of course, shaking hands.

We arrived home after landing at Marseilles before spending a day in Paris, where we bought some very dashing hats. We got back into the gentle, rather sluggish life at Barton, until in the autumn a message came from Eric, saying he had broken a brief engagement, been ill and would like our company again. We sailed by the British India line from the London docks. It was hard to believe we were in a ship as we watched a bowler-hatted man open gates for her to slide though with seemingly inches to spare, turn somehow and still looking as if she was in a street, get into the Thames.

A month later we were in Laikipia. We had a more sociable time

Eric ponders how to get his car out of a mud hole.

Crossing the Pesi River above the swamp in the 1920s.

as we now had a T-model Ford with a box body. It went quite well, though I frequently arrived at the end of the journey with my hair in two plaits, Eric having used up all the hairpins making repairs to the car. I was once nearly knocked unconscious when I hit the wooden roof, although I had my topee on.

Some of our neighbours decided with us that the rivers Narok and Pesi should be stocked with trout. We made up a party and drove the 50 miles across the plains to Nanyuki, where there are many small rivers coming off Mt Kenya, all well stocked with both the rainbow and brown variety. We stayed at the hotel putting in a long day of fishing. A large withy basket was made, weighed down in the water with stones. Each of us had a young African lad acting as a ghillie. When we landed a fish, it was his job to dash and place it in the basket before it died. We had a good catch, so even though the water rose in the night, and the bigger ones leaped out, we were able to load them up the next morning into *debes*. There was no need to stop and change the water as the jolting aerated it. By the afternoon they were in the top reaches of our rivers where they flourished.

At this time Jack McDonogh was stationed at Rumuruti as veterinary officer, going about seeing cattle were dipped and injected against East Coast Fever and Rinderpest. He had been stationed at Isiolo and had the pick of the ponies the Somalis had brought down.

Later we went to Nanyuki, this time to camp in some all-thatch huts just above the race-course. We spent the holiday fishing and training Jack's string of horses before the gymkhana. This meant hacking them up and down hills to muscle them up. They were delightful little creatures. I only knew one standing at fourteen hands, but they were very quick on their feet and jumped well. They had no shoulders to speak of and had a disconcerting way of putting their heads down when galloping. There seemed to be nothing between you and the hard, hard earth of Africa, especially if your mount jinked round an ant-heap. Still, they were plucky and tough. On one occasion they re-enacted Kipling's story of the Maltese Cat, when the Fifth KAR went down to Nairobi from Meru and beat all the better mounted teams at polo.

Being so near the lovely mountain, we longed to climb it. The great crags were for expert, roped climbers, but surely we could get to the snow-line? As yet there were no tracks, but Raymond Hook was used to spending much of his time on its slopes, so we asked him to be our guide. Our party - Cicely, Jack, Mary Luxford and I - arranged to meet him above the road at Timau, where he would have riding and pack ponies complete with camping gear all ready to start in the early morning, A number of people have written about Raymond, a

Jack McDonogh on his polo pony Mandarin at Ndaiga in the 1920s.

donnish man who looked like a disreputable cowboy. Though good company, his exploits had a zany quality, ensuring you were in for entertainment and danger.

The first thing to happen immediately after we moved off, was a large mare acting as a pack horse appeared to go mad. She leaped about, scattering tins of food, plates and cutlery all over the place. She was, we were told, called Amelia the Murderess, as she had killed two grooms. Raymond was surprised at her misbehaving for, he said, "She was very good at carrying bales of hay. It must be the rattle." Our equipment grew steadily less as we went our way. Our route ran up the crest of a ridge, deep gullies falling away on each side of the narrow crest. Here we were likely to meet a rhino. "It will either charge up the mountain or down," Raymond explained. 'Or at us. So the odds are in our favour!" Jack rode ahead with his gun, then Mary and myself. Cicely, following, roused the rhino. We had a good view of it, red as India rubber, turning neatly as a pig and plunging down the hill, nearly knocking Cicely's pony over, whilst Raymond waved it away with his hat. Cicely galloped up looking white. She said her one thought had been that she might lose her only hair-slide.

The next bit was through forest and then thick bamboo. Our way had to be cut and we lay on our pony's necks, looking down at the

Jack McDonogh with Cicely and Joan at Ndaiga in 1928.

steaming elephant dung. This, I thought, is exactly like being a rabbit in a hay field full of dogs – no tree to climb or anywhere to hide. I did not like it a bit. At last clear of the bamboo we came to open forest, where yellow raspberry plants and everlasting flowers grew. Then came the giant heather on very bleak moorland. Our tents were pitched. We were about 14,000 feet up and it drizzled. Next day we rode over tussocks of course grass. I fell off and pulled a muscle. The ponies stopped to puff every few yards and one nearly fell over a scree. Then the clouds came down and we voted we'd had enough. "We could find a cave," suggested Raymond, but this did not appeal to us. So we returned to camp. The altitude made me feel sick and gave me a headache, but Mary and Cicely became ravenous, eating masses of condensed milk and golden syrup, to me a dreadful sight.

The rest was without adventures. As a safari it was more interesting then enjoyable. But it was worth it for the god-like view of immense distances, like a gold and blue ocean where mountains rose up like islands.

Back in Nanyuki we met a couple noted for their staying power. Their technique was to arrive in a car with a faulty engine, which somehow could never be made to run. The Man who Stayed to Dinner had nothing on them. Legend had it that they lingered so long with a district police officer that, in despair, he went on safari. When he got back, he found that they were still there. Being in camp we missed this treat; our only experience was when Jack was fixing up his fishing tackle one afternoon and the husband came up mumbling

Nanyuki in 1927.

Eric Booth on a visit to Nairobi in 1927.

something about "Hook." The association of ideas made Jack hand him a fishhook. "Thank you," he said, carefully putting it in his wallet, "I really need Raymond Hook."

Our upcountry gymkhanas surpassed any other form of racing for me. You were running ponies you had picked – or trusted a knowledgeable friend to pick – from the bunch of sore-covered near-skeletons that hobbled along after their terrible journey over the wastes of the Northern Frontier. Then you took them home and hoped they would not die of the dreaded horse sickness; if they pulled through it took a year at least for them to recover fully. They were then valuable as being 'salted.' They also had to get over the rough handling from their Somali or Ethiopian owners. Some had Arab blood in them, and those from the Boran tribe were popular. Also, these had been used to drinking milk, which was a help in regaining fitness.

After some months rumours would begin to circulate. Major Baynes had picked a chestnut, absolutely unbeatable over a mile. This

109

was obviously untrue because you had picked a better pony, and you had a cream one that jumped like a stag. So you worked and dreamed and entered your pony, catch weight 11 stone 7 lbs, trusting whoever was riding to get his weight down, as that meant rider and saddle of course. Jack McDonogh would just leave off eating and was lucky in having a horribly uncomfortable two-pound saddle. He proudly wore his family's racing colours, worn by his father and famous Great Uncle Allan, who rode the favourite in the first Grand National.

Only the other day I discovered that bothersome word 'meek' in the New Testament means 'broken in' as with a horse, knowledge which has been of tremendous comfort and inspiration to me. Any of us who watch those Horse Trials on television, must gasp at the terrifying obstacles horse and rider tackle. No wild horse in its senses would take them on, but a meek horse, trusting its rider, does, and does with joy. I know some people are sentimental about the poor horses in a steeplechase, and I wish they could watch one being trained. Ours were driven in long runs up to a low jump with high wings to prevent it running out. Time and time again, with rolling eyes and snorts, it would refuse, then in utter desperation it would take the jump.

A very inelegant scramble it would be, but once over there was a transformation. The ears went up and it would turn and look at the horrible barrier and positively dance and whinny. Every muscle and hair saying, "I've done it! I've jumped, I'm a steeplechaser." The next time it would fly over like a swallow.

I remember two special events that holiday. The major one was that Cicely and Jack became engaged. A very minor event happened on a hot afternoon, when I decided to have a bath. It was one of those horrid green canvas saucers, which slop water all over the floor. Scrubbing away, I realized the hut was becoming much less dark – in fact windows were appearing on every side. The hut was being devoured in a matter of seconds by fifteen ponies.

Cicely's husband-to-be was Jack McDonogh, who had served in West and East Africa, being one of two men to hold commissions in the Royal Army Medical Corps (RAMC) without being doctors. He had been a medical student in Dublin and rather than be a Doctor in

Eric treating a cow at Barton in 1927.

Eric branding cattle at Barton in 1928.

Ireland, he had thrown his hand in and went abroad. Anyone in South Africa who knew the least bit about medicine was roped in to look after the troops, and a very good doctor he was, having a quick eye for diagnosis, understanding the African physique, and being adaptable to shortages. At one time during World War I he had a battalion, a small hospital and a labour camp in his care and was delirious with malaria most evenings. Hammis bin Baraka, his Swahili valet, would collect him, sponge him down, and get him onto parade next day. At last he left South Tanganyika on a stretcher in a dying condition but after a time in Kenya was sent as a medical officer to Jubaland, that big desert country now included in Somalia.

Hammis had been left with two shillings in his pocket but he tracked Jack down and joined him, standing by him loyally through those troubled times when the Mad Mullah was murdering KAR officers and his own people with ghastly impartiality.

In 1920 Jack had his first real leave, arriving in Ireland when the Troubles were at their height. He was both surprised and annoyed

Hammis at Ndaiga in 1928.

112

when the hotel in Dublin where his family had always stayed refused to put him up. Even when he pointed out that he was used to sleeping on the floor, they still told him to go to another hotel. He was in mufti but his luggage was marked with his rank and regiment. Next morning he found that every officer in the hotel he had first called at, had been dragged from his bed and shot. The west of Ireland was just as unhappy a place, and his beloved mother had died and his father was an old broken man. Moreover, a specialist gave him two years if he lived cautiously. So he went to London and spent his savings meeting his old army friends, racing and having a tremendous spree. Then, finding himself still alive and nearly broke, he decided to return to Kenya and get a job. On the quay at Mombasa was Hammis who said, "Jambo, Bwana, where are your keys?"

The day after Cicely and Jack's engagement was made known I ran into Charlie Maynleer in Nanyuki High Street. Charlie traded ponies, bringing them down from Ethiopia. As usual, he was drunk, and on seeing me he burst into tears, a habit of his when moved. He pumped my hand up and down vigorously and said, "Take an Old Man's blessing."

"It's not I that's engaged," I said. "It's my sister."

"Never mind," said he, almost crossly. "Take an Old Man's blessing!"

I could only reply, "Thank you very much."

A short while after this, on his way north, he called in at some great friends of ours who lived on the fringe of the settled area. It was evening and he rode up on his old white horse, wearing a purple dressing gown split up the back for riding, clasping his banjo and very tight. Too full of drink to fancy dinner, he sat strumming during the meal and afterwards said he must go back to his camp. Billy and Norah begged him to stay overnight as there were many lions about, as well as rhino. He said he must go, so his horse was saddled. It then struck him that, as Norah was going down to Nairobi next day in order to give birth to her baby in a civilised place, this was an occasion when a speech was called for. So, taking her by the hand – and probably crying, Norah did not say – he declaimed, "Mrs B, if I don't see you again...If I do not see you again...Well, if I do not see you again...It doesn't matter very much does it?" Then he mounted and rode away.

This story almost makes me cry, because he did not see her again. Weeks later a Somali from the Non-Combatant-Corps (NCC), who had just been paid off, came to his tent and called, "Bwana Charlie." When Charlie stepped out, he shot him. There seemed to be no known reason – unless the man was feeling freed from the restraint of the army and was fanatical enough to believe killing an infidel was a passport to paradise.

CHAPTER 8

Adventures in Nanyuki

Norah and Billy Beale came to be neighbours of ours after Cicely and Jack settled in that district, and very dear friends they were, in spite of their having an astoundingly bad cook. They loved him dearly and were quite open about his failings, urging us at dinner to compete in making the soup drinkable: some cream and Worcestershire sauce, and what about a dash of tabasco or sherry? It really was sad that collective indigestion forced us to leave earlier than we had meant. We would arrive loaded up with food, saying our cook had happened to bake a great many more loaves than usual and we did not like them wasted. They were accepted with joy and put aside for the future, and the wet, concrete-like stuff did its deadly work. Sadder still was the Christmas we spent there. Norah announced that a small Stilton cheese and a plum pudding had arrived from England. Next day the dogs got into the larder and devoured them both. Very replete and impenitent they looked.

Norah was full of good stories. One was how, one night, she had heard a lot of stamping and blundering about outside the bedroom, where her small precious rose garden lay. There being an old superannuated bull on the farm, which was apt to roam, she rose up and grabbing the only weapon at hand, namely a coat hangar, went out and thumped it well on its backside and pushed it into a convenient shed, shutting it up for the rest of the night. In the morning she discovered that she had dealt with the new Friesian bull, an animal so dangerous that it usually lived behind a high stockade, and was

Barton in Rumuruti in about 1928.

handled with the greatest caution. So trying, as she said, not to be able to claim extreme bravery.

A really good story, and I mean good, in its true sense, was when their dear cook turned up one morning with that strange pewter like greyness an African goes when really ill or upset. On being asked what the matter was he said that he had been cursed and was about to die. This was dreadful and both Billy and Norah tried to assure him that this need not be. Their efforts met with complete failure, and in two days, Norah said that there was no question about it; the man was dying. She fell back on every bit of faith and imagination she had and then took action. Waiting until there would be no interruption, she arranged the Bible and other large books on a table along with a candle and other things she felt necessary, and called Cook from his hut. When he came, she told him truthfully that she had consulted many wise books, had prayed, and now knew exactly what to do to remove the curse. First, he must reveal the name, clan and dwelling place of the one who invoked the curse. This he did and Norah wrote them down on a large sheet of paper. She carefully folded it in three and sealed it three times with sealing wax. Then she put the paper into one of his hands and the candle in the other, and bade him follow her down to a quiet corner of the orchard. Now, he must stand on the piece of paper, whilst she walked round him three times saying the

Lord's Prayer out loud. She had never prayed more fervently as she knew she was up against the Powers of Darkness. This done, the man burnt the paper and trampled the ashes into the earth, finishing the rite by swigging a dose of medicine composed of castor oil, whisky and Worcestershire sauce. "Now," she said, "the curse is lifted, *Kabisa* – Absolutely," and, thank God, it was. Mpishi was cured from that minute.

Jack was now stationed at Isiolo where there was a large concrete dip and very little else. His job as veterinary officer was to see that every head of cattle brought down by the Somalis was dipped before entering the more inhabited parts of Kenya. A very small charge was made per head, but there was a constant game of hide-and-seek in the bush as the herdsmen tried to evade him. Jack pointed out that he kept his sixteen bore by his bed and being extremely quick with a gun, would certainly get two of them, should they think of visiting him during the night. Moreover the KAR up at Meru would be delighted to come down like a pack of wolves should there be any mishap. The Somalis quite understood and behaved amicably.

One day when they were being deliberately slow, making the work more exhausting than usual, they came to announce smugly that the work was done and they would pay their fee. Jack pointed out that not all the animals had been dipped. There were still the donkeys. The Somalis argued that donkeys are not dipped. They would be this evening, said Jack, and spent a pleasurable time watching half a dozen kicking, biting, donkeys going through the filthy mixture with at least four struggling Somalis attached to each. Instead of murdering him on the spot, they took it in good part. Another point in his favour was that if Bwana Mac approved of a pony the price went up automatically.

It was this year that a cousin of ours came out to look round for work. He had been employed by a firm in Nigeria, and hoped to learn the language and get a managing job, or a small farm. He had come from an unhappy home, survived the war, and was a thorn in the flesh. He seemed to have no fear, doing crazy things such as galloping after zebra while firing his rifle, with the reins round his neck. He was generally discourteous and, if told that Africans particularly disliked

Fording the Sirima River in about 1927.

some gesture or word, would promptly go out and try it on, coming back to recount with joy how upset or frightened he had made them. We should have combined forces and somehow shanghaied him onto a ship leaving the country, as he was impervious to hints. I went about saying I was astounded that no-one had landed him a real facer.

Only a few days after Cicely and I reached England, the *Manchester Guardian* had the headlines that this man had been ambushed and hacked to pieces. Then I realised the awful fact that Jesus Christ had said that whoever goes about thinking hate and murder is the same as he who does the deed. The Africans might have been more handy with a spear and panga than I, but we all had been exasperated by him. They would be hanged. My punishment was to go to his weeping mother and sit whilst she wailed over and over again, "He was the best boy in the world."

Cicely and Jack were married in St Martin-in-the-Fields. It had been her church when she worked in London. Jack's beautiful spirited sister, Ina, came over from Galway for the event. It was she who, back in Ireland, on hearing that anyone wearing red, white and blue, would be shot, went to the races with the biggest cockade she could make, routed a band who held up her dogcart at gun point, telling them they were only after her binoculars, and addressing them by their names, calling them silly boys and threatening that she would tell the local butcher, who was their leader, what an ill-mannered lot they were.

Fairly soon after the wedding we were on our way back to Kenya. I didn't question that I should go with them; everyone seemed to take it for granted, as Cicely wasn't very strong or domesticated. Strange that in those days there was a dividing line between those who were or weren't. Not that I was particularly skilled that way myself, but I wasn't clever, and did like food and comfort.

We travelled back again in the British India Line. It was an unremarkable voyage except for the incident of the Forceful Female. She was the niece of an elderly couple and a few years older than us. Somehow the idea was conjured up, in the Red Sea of all places, that it would be awfully jolly to act charades. Not simple spontaneous charades

Joan Booth,
the bridesmaid.

119

acted on the spot, but organized. One scene would be Burke addressing Parliament, so Jack, being Irish, must be he. Another scene was to be Canute commanding the waves. The waves would be some of us rolling about the decks under travelling rugs. (I said it was the Red Sea!) By the evening the passengers were becoming near hysterical. For once I was brave, and catching a chap who was immensely popular with her, I begged him to do something about it, as there would either be mutiny or mass suicide. He did. Her idea of charades was dropped and the Red Sea almost became chilly. Whether there was a happy ending I do not know, but this did prove he could manage her. What did happen was that, at Kilindini, her trunk of lovely clothes was dropped into the water, at which she gallantly laughed, and he proposed to her.

Hammis was waiting for us, and after the usual pause in Nairobi we set out for the farm Cicely and Jack had acquired. It lay in the Loldaiga hills north of Nanyuki, and was bought from an elderly doctor who wished to retire to the coast.

The McDonoghs had a six-cylinder Chrysler car, a big strong thing with a Cape cart hood. It had an excellent engine and as the rains were on, we set out with chains on the wheels. We went by way of Nyeri and I remember it most vividly. Nowadays the road is tarmacked and one gets there in three hours or so. This trip we averaged thirty miles a day, and a long day at that. The engine never gave out. It would push mud almost to the top of the radiator. Then it had to be scraped away whilst someone took a tyre lever and chipped the congealed stuff from between the chassis and wheels. The first day was spent getting to the Blue Posts at Thika, some 30 odd miles and comparatively easy, compared with the very long second day. The road runs serpent-like up and down the steep valleys of Kikuyu country. This journey was made longer when we met an askari beside the wreckage of a bridge over a flooded river. He told us to retrace our steps - and they were for the most part steps - seven miles, and then branch off to find a bridge up-stream, which, though rickety, might get us over the water. On our asking him if he had turned many cars back, he positively beamed. "Many, many cars," he said. We never discovered who had posted him there instead of at the diversion.

A military parade at Rumuruti on 11 November 1927
to celebrate Remembrance Day.

It was nightfall when we got to Fort Hall. We were put up by the District Officer. He was a friend of Jack's and, of course, used to putting up wayfarers, but as he had only one spare room I was allotted an outhouse, with the comfort of a sentry outside who, poor man, had a hacking cough. I was even more glad to have a mosquito net because the hut swithered with hundreds and hundreds of bats. It is all very well to know that they have sensitive noses and never hit you, but I do not like bats, however interesting they may be. So I shoved my one piece of furniture against the door - it was a packing case - and dived under the net most thankfully.

Another long struggle the next day took us to Nyeri where there was a hotel. The fourth day got us out of the valleys and through the more open country to Nanyuki. Here many small rivers flow from the mountain, so people shook their heads and said we might possibly get to the farm, which was fifteen miles away, on a horse. We rested there four days waiting for these waters to subside.

We were in country we knew; the post office with its pinky white thornless rose, which had lost its name long ago but flourishes all over the country and is known as 'the Post Office Rose'; the butcher's shop run by a colonel, who would ride round looking very dapper indeed, cheerfully taking orders; the Indian store and another run by a terrifying major's wife, and even a little office, which produced an upcountry newspaper. As yet the club had only a bar and a large wooden hut where we danced during the gymkhana - dances lasting until dawn, when our partners would get their ponies out and play ten-a-side polo in evening dress.

Outside Nanyuki was a stretch of black cotton soil, stuff which sets like concrete when dry, but when wet turns to black bottomless porridge. In those days before the Public Works Department tried ineffectually to drain the road by digging deep trenches on either side, so forcing you to stick to it, you just took to the open country, trying not to break your springs or your sump on a tree-root. All over the area there would be craters where cars had dug themselves down to the chassis, to be pulled out by ox-teams. It was this bit of 'road' which sent a man walking back to Nanyuki after two-and-a-half days, leaving his big Willys-Knight 14 miles out of town. As he refreshed himself at the store he was faced by a full-page advertisement in the *East African Standard*, which proudly announced that somebody had crossed the United States in a Willys-Knight in a record-breaking number of hours.

Our road to the farm lay most of the way through thick forest and over several small rivers, some having wooden bridges. The house had been built in a clearing, near the river, the better part of the farm running back into the hills in a wide waterless valley, later to have a pump and a dam, making it excellent for stock. It was a delightful homestead with numbers of thatched buildings surrounded by a garden and tall blue gum trees. A water furrow most ingeniously made to travel over wooden flumes brought our supply from a mile upstream right to the house. There was a paddock for the ponies and about twenty acres of cleared land where we hoped to grow maize - a false hope as it was ravaged by baboons in the daytime and by buffalo at night.

The stream was well stocked with brown trout - one obligingly came down the furrow to the kitchen door. You had to be careful. The only time I have known the terror of being bushed was when I took the car to a place where the river ran almost in a circle. Beginning to fish at one end of this horseshoe, I got about half way round before deciding it was too hot and bright for the fish to rise. Taking a short cut back, I had only gone a few yards when I was both lost and stuck in an entanglement of thorns. Although I could hear the running water it seemed a very long time until, breathless and dripping with sweat, I fought my way to the bank and waded downstream to the car. I had always considered myself to have a good sense of direction, and was used to woods. The whole episode lasted only half an hour or so, but quite long enough and taught me a lesson.

The elderly couple who were leaving were packing. The doctor left some of his things, including drugs in a store, which was as well as they saved Cicely's life a few months later. His wife was having a bad time. A brilliant woman and an excellent gardener, she was that strange thing – a miser. Every piece of paper, string or cotton reel had been hoarded, and she had the heartbreak of leaving them behind. Although the kitchen shelves were loaded with dozens of eggs, she was in real anguish at having to feed us, working out that by scrambling them she could use one less. She had nearly killed her daughters with overwork as she would not employ anyone to get firewood or work in the garden but made them spend their time doing this heavy work or making cakes for sale. Great tales were told of their romantic escapes to marry the men of their choice. When she left she was busily making an evening bag out of the plush rescued from the doctor's old silk hat.

We settled down in this beautiful place. Jack continued to work at Isiolo and would ride the 40 miles to join us at weekends. The cattle produced good cross-bred calves. The cream went twice a week to the Co-op dairy by pack ponies. A couple of the younger men would take them the eight-mile journey. They were allowed to ride back, provided they rode gently and they were forbidden to take the dogs as there were many baboons on the way. With four hands and dreadful teeth they are death to a dog if they catch it. Then when Jack was at home the convoy returned with the ponies ridden to exhaustion and all the dogs but one killed. He was too angry to take action himself so sent the lads in to the police station with a report, asking that they should get a good beating. The answer came back

*Eric and Joan with
Jack McDonogh
and Cicely by the
Ewaso Nyiro River.*

that, as they were young, they could not have a beating without the consent of their parents. The parents lived some sixty miles away, so the police sent them back.

We were kept busy looking after the garden where there was a constant war with the little mouse birds. With their parrot beaks they could eat the fruit whilst still green and hard. It was a joy to have vegetables in plenty and the two fruits the birds could not attack, granadilla and lemons. The bird life was a delight. Golden crested cranes curtsied to each other. We had kingfishers, and collared starlings, as well as very tiny neat little birds, deep plum or turquoise blue, which looked for crumbs at the door. Then there was the silly-looking but beautiful blue, green and rose turaco, flopping about in the trees, and gazing at you with golden eyes.

Earlier at Rumuruti a large flock of storks flying south landed on the open plain one afternoon, at half past two. They stood in a clump as if in earnest talk, then made off two by two. All evening and next morning they could be seen in couples ranging about the farm feasting off grasshoppers. Then at the same hour they were on the place where they landed. Again they had a ten-minute chat and took off. It would have been wonderful to have ringed them. Now swallows and bee-eaters are being ringed and traced. Those which migrate from Kenya go to Central and Eastern Europe, while some local birds change their territory in the country. The place for game birds was Isiolo; francolin, spurfowl and various kinds of guinea fowl pottered about as if in a well-stocked farmyard, and the little sand grouse came down to take one sip at the water pans and jinked away back to their desert homes.

There is an African story that the spurfowl were discontented when they were created. They told the Creator that they wished to be as large and handsome as the guinea fowl. He agreed to do this but during the process of change the Europeans turned up. This so disorganised everything that the poor birds were forgotten. Now they are called francolin and can be heard in the bush crying, "Get on with the work!"

Whilst at Isiolo, Jack had a remarkable pointer called Ranger. He not only pointed game but would retrieve and also drive birds over the gun. A friend named Robin, a notoriously bad shot, took him out to get something for the pot. He came back empty-handed, saying that Ranger had driven birds over from the left, then from the right, then cast round and drove them over him. After that he gave Robin a long sad look and put up a hare, then he went home. He was one of those dogs that smile, especially if he had been eating hen's eggs, to which he was addicted. He would come in wagging his tail and grin, unaware of the telltale marks on his chops. You couldn't do much with such a charmer, but scold him. He would then look crestfallen, and go off to see if another lay-away had obliged him with a snack.

About this time Cicely and I went to stay at Isiolo. It is on the edge of the desert country, where a steady hot wind blows all day long. While there we were asked to tea by Jack's only neighbour, who lived five miles away. Rattray, now a middle-aged man, had left Scotland to wander about the world working with horses. Now he was catching the big Grevy's zebra, with a view to using them in districts where horses cannot live. They took a long time to train, but he had four pulling a trap. Motor vehicles, and their high price, caused them to be used in circuses and zoos. Rattray's work was slowed up because a few years earlier he had a fight with a leopard. He only got away by half strangling it. Even so, the leopard was able to turn inside its skin as a cat can, and had bitten through his wrists. A long period with blood poisoning had left him with weakened hands.

He picked me up in his battered old box body car. I had on a particularly pretty blue silk dress, and maybe going out with this John Wayne-like person caused me to look rather pleased with myself, because his first suggestion was to go to the end of his bomas to see if there were any lion about. I was glad there were none, but he shot a Burchell's zebra for dog meat. Asking me to hold the hind leg, still twitching, he removed it with his Bowie knife, a bloody business, and quite heavy to heave into the car. On the way back he said he needed meat himself, stopped the car, strolled out onto an open plain and dropped a half-grown oryx. Calling me, he handed me his enormous rifle – a .303 is not heavy enough for really big game – and told me to shoot the cow, should she charge, whilst he went for the car. I wonder if I looked as green as I felt. It seemed a very long time before he drove up, whilst I revolved slowly, keeping an eye on her as with her yard-long bayonet horns, she revolved round me in much too small a circle. Then there was the longer struggle to get the big carcass into the car, and on to our tea party. Dear Rattray! He took me to a dance once in Nairobi a few years later. He was a trifle lit up, and chaparoned me like a Victorian matron, making me feel as if I was made of Venetian glass and fiercely bidding me not to go near sundry men who he considered to be 'awful rascals!'

Cicely's miscarriage happened providentially on the farm at the weekend when, by pure chance, two doctors happened to be in Meru, 50 miles away. They came over to look after her, so I had no nursing to do. The only place where she could be kept warm was in the kitchen where there was a wood burning stove. It was the oldest hut of the lot, with an earth floor and a constant shower of white ants from the thatched roof, kippered dark brown by smoke. Sterilisation was reduced to a minimum, with no ill results. Our friends broke into the old doctor's store and found the necessary drugs. She picked up remarkably quickly.

We had two great pets in our ponies – Mick and Pat. They had been reared by an Arab and were very affectionate, putting their heads through windows to have a friendly word. In the evening they would pretend to play polo together, tearing up and down and shouldering each other off an imaginary ball. The others, which had known the hideous cruelty of the Ethiopian bit, took longer to settle, though Jack, who knew the old trick of breathing into their nostrils, could do anything he liked with them.

Once a very curious thing happened. A friend far away near the border wrote to say he was sending two ponies down to Nairobi and would be grateful if they could rest for a week on the farm, before continuing their long journey. They arrived one evening, were rubbed down, stabled and fed. Next morning they met our ponies and a mule. Somehow they conveyed to ours that they were on safari, because within an hour they began to process, nose to tail. In and out round the smaller huts and the central garden, then along a veranda they plodded, with our three ponies and the mule following suit. With heads down and taking no notice of us they kept exactly to the same route until noon, when they broke off and went to graze. They never repeated the performance, so perhaps our lot convinced them that it was not part of their routine.

Lions were still a nuisance. We wished to keep the cattle in paddocks by night, so that they could feed. Our lion trap came into action, but Hammis had a narrow escape when one lion was shot in the side of its head and stunned. The farm hands were joyfully singing about its death when one bold fellow pulled its tail, whereupon it got up and charged. Because of its wound it missed Hammis by a couple of feet. "My heart died within me," he said. A young Turkana bravely headed the animal off, whilst someone ran to the house for Jack's gun - Hammis was able to shoot it. It was a very close run thing for him as he had his leg in plaster due to a bad fall.

It seems dreadful in these days to think that we regarded lions and leopards as vermin and were happy when African neighbours, who had smallholdings, trapped and killed leopards, bringing us the skins, for which they asked five shillings.

CHAPTER 9

Cicely's Baby is Born and Eric Marries Phyllis Armitage

W hen Cicely's baby was on the way we took a house in Nairobi. It belonged to a doctor who was going to Scotland on holiday, leaving his locum to stay with us.

Baby Mary arrived safely and quickly. Cicely played bridge with three doctors until eleven o'clock, a good influence, perhaps, as Mary was born next morning. The nurse taking the case was a strange woman; maybe the tragedy of losing her husband shortly before affected her. Even in those days we thought it fussy to forbid all visitors for a week and insist on a month in bed. What was worse, no fruit or vegetables were to be eaten, apart from potatoes, with awful warnings as to what happened to babies whose mothers indulged in greens or fruit. Mary's natural cries were put down to my having put three strawberries on a rice pudding, and Cicely grew more liverish and spotty until I went over to her doctor's wife, who had trained with nurse, to ask if all this was necessary. She said that in their hospital the first meal the mothers had was a good plate of Scotch broth. To our joy, Doctor's first words on next looking in, were, "Now then Mrs Mac, what about some fruit?" Nurse looked as if he had said cyanide.

A day or so later the nurse became ill and left. Neither Cicely nor I had coped with a baby before, so we thought Mary was a very fragile

Jack and Cicely McDonogh with their daughter Mary at 11 weeks of age in Nairobi.

object. Our textbook was, as to thousands of mothers, by Dr Truby King. He laid down laws such as that babies should be fed four-hourly and never picked up between whiles, except for nappy changing. Any soft-heartedness would cause physical and psychological ruin, which was true as far as we were concerned. At last we decided that baby should be fed at three-hour intervals, whereupon she flourished, and thank heaven, slept through the nights. We were still apt to panic, being sure that convulsions or something equally dire would happen, so it was quite a time before we learnt that babies are tough and intelligent.

By this time I had lost my heart once and for all. The locum, Sandy, who was small and wiry with blue eyes and light step had stolen my heart away. After doctoring in Singapore, he had taken his F.R.C. S. in

Joan lost her heart to Dr JH 'Sandy' Tennant, but they were unable to marry. Here Sandy Tennant is holding his dogs Judy and Toby in 1928.

Edinburgh, parted from his wife, and come to Kenya to make a new life. I felt his saying he was a hedonist and his flirting was an anodyne to pain. Once only he kissed me with passion, awakening all the passion in me, so that from the very depths I cried, "This is my man, my love." Deeper still was the necessity as a woman to be able to stand in the open and say before his people and my people and our God, that I was taking a mate and a companion for life. Nothing, not even the physical longing, which tore me, could alter that. So we remained good friends and wrote companionable letters to each other for years.

Doctoring was tough going in those days. For example, a wire came for Sandy to say that in Sotik, not far from Lake Victoria, a settler had appendicitis. The rains were on, so all along the road people stood by with cars or oxen to get Sandy through. Six cars were wrecked in the process and, on arriving, he had to wait for an hour for his hands to become steady before operating on a table, by the light of hurricane lamps.

While we were in Nairobi, Eric met Phyllis Armitage, who had been the first Health Visitor in Britain, working in Battersea. She had been lured out by the Governor's wife, who had painted an imaginary picture of a large hostel and clinic for children. She was sorely disappointed on finding the Lady Northey Home, which was a tiny place, where sometimes one or two children might stay a few days.

Cicely McDonogh holding her baby Mary as Joan (centre) and Phyllis Armitage, the nurse, look on. When Eric came to see his new niece, he met Phyllis and the two fell in love.

The problem of what to do was solved when she and Eric became engaged and were married within a few weeks. They lived on the Laikipia farm for a short while, and when their daughter Celia was little, they moved to a farm running parallel with the McDonogh's, leaving the old farm to be used as a ranch. Its lack of water fitted it for this, rather than for dairy produce.

Before they moved, I went over to stay with them for a week or two and while there we had an earthquake. It was a fairly mild one, though the timber house swayed about and creaked considerably. For

Eric Booth married Phyllis Armitage. Joan Booth acted as the maid of honour, while Dr Sandy Tennant was the best man.

a week after one would be wakened by the bed shuddering. Cicely's home did not collapse either. She realised what was happening and called to Jack to take the baby outside. He thought it was an elephant or perhaps a rhino barging into the wall, and saw no reason to go out to confront it with a baby in his arms. What was very nasty for them was that when they looked towards the mountains they saw a dull glow. Kenya's peak is the core of an old volcano and next morning a car came through with people from well up its slopes. It was good news to learn they were not fleeing from an eruption, and that the glow was only a forest fire.

Earthquakes are disagreeable things, even when they are not disastrous. The fact that there is nowhere to go, or no one to blame, outrages a person, who naturally looks for both. To live where they constantly take place must be terrible and I only hope is compensated by people being more than ordinarily good neighbours. I am yet to be convinced that there is no earthquake weather. A strange, still, onimous feeling, with a kind of brassy light hangs about. That shifting plates of rock, deep down, can affect the atmosphere seems nonsense, but whenever there has been a bit of heaving and shuddering, I maintain you get that feeling beforehand.

When Mary was nine months old, we sailed home on an Italian

Joan Booth with her new sister-in-law Phyllis
at Barton with their horse Tinker in 1928.

liner, very comfortable and full of interest. There was a British Colonel's wife we knew slightly who chose to travel second class. She engaged in a voyage-long war with her three Italian cabin-mates, as to the porthole being open. We met her one morning off to do battle with the Captain armed with a plate of butter. She really was one of those who spoiled for a fight.

Also there was the distraught Englishwoman found wandering below decks. On being asked what was up she cried, "I want the steward to come and translate the taps." My Italian is practically non-existent, so I learnt four new words, as there was salt and fresh water as well as hot and cold. Then there was a splendidly ridiculous scene when one of us started to roar for marmalade at breakfast. As *marmelata* means jam, he was brought every rare and exotic jam the stewards could find, only to cry, "No! Marmalade, dammit," until somebody took the chance that this man wanted that most despised orange stuff.

Mary was a huge success because she did not cry and really did begin to be a bit spoilt through being constantly danced round the deck by her admirers. She had a splendid evening when, after a film – we had a few all with terribly tragic endings, and were told that such scenes had to be made to satisfy the Italian market – we found her feasting on sugar biscuits with the barman. I think the stewardess had brought her up for him to admire. On other nights we would find both stewardess and baby fast asleep after a concert of spirited Neapolitan songs.

We had royalty on board in the person of the Duke of the Abruzzi, a pleasant courteous man doomed to sit at a table apart, with two ancient Contessas of American birth. When we called at Massawa, a tremendous band played to greet the gold-encrusted super Fascists who came aboard. That was a morning when our duke retired to his cabin.

Much less happy was the small zoo of animals going to an exhibition in Turin, and some Somalis. Probably they had never seen the sea, but at Mogadishu they were rowed out in lighters and then thrown onto a square of tarpaulin which was let down to be hauled up and swung aboard. The women in their rich finery, screaming, kicking

Phyllis Booth developing film at Barton, where she had her own darkroom.

Eric and Phyllis hosted Dr Sandy Tennant for Christmas in 1928.

and biting, obviously felt that this was a fate worse than death, and the following weeks spent in the open well deck cannot have done anything towards happy colonial relations. Presumably they were sent to the exhibition to take part in a charming model village scene, at which the public would gawp.

Only a few years before this Italian Somaliland had its frontier moved southwards, so as to include the coast town of Kismayu and a large piece of what had been the British Northern Frontier District of Kenya. Soon afterwards our friends, the Beals, were travelling in an Italian ship. Its Captain described to them the incident: "When we took over the place we arrived with one cruiser and two destroyers, a brass band, an Admiral and a General and many soldiers. And what did we find? Mr Horne and one walking stick!"

This may be a slight distortion of the truth. There is a true story, though, of how a band of Somalis, having a husbandless grandmother in their party, decided to abandon her in the desert. Her twelve-year-old grandson protested, and having no success, announced he would take her to Kismayu where she would be cared for. Possibly he had inherited a camel or donkeys, for he set out with her and his small sister and brought her two hundred miles to the place, and asked to see the District Commissioner, who did indeed look after them.

We arrived in the spring, spending the summer at Barton where baby Mary was a great delight to her grandparents. After a brief holiday in Ireland, the McDonoghs returned to Kenya, leaving me at home, as the parents needed me. As the train to Tilbury drew out of the station, I waved goodbye and felt the deep churning pain of any female animal on losing its young.

CHAPTER 10

Back to England

Mother was having frequent attacks of heart trouble and exhaustion. In those days the care of the elderly consisted of plenty of rest and good nourishing meals, contrary to the present day staple diet and lots of exercise line. Still, when she felt well she was perfectly ready to scramble onto the Roman wall and twist her leg badly trying to jump off it.

Always there was the dread of Connie leaving her seaside flat and coming home, when she stormed at us all, crying out for more affection. Appeasement was the name for the long useless struggle to keep the peace with someone who said she resented us all; Father and Mother because they were wrapped up in each other, and the rest of us because we existed. She said, with that dreadful honesty these people have, "Here I am in hell, walking round and round myself."

For anyone not involved there were moments of comedy. Often when her friends came to stay, and having been kept up to the small hours listening to her wrongs, we would be lectured to as to how she was misunderstood, with advice as to our behaviour. Within a few days these friends would leave in a fury of exasperation.

One super-comedy was when we were leaving the hotel at Les Diablerets. Connie was unable to get her clothes into her boxes. Time was running out, and after repeatedly folding and wedging there was still a pile of stuff to carry to where the cases waited on a sleigh. It was humiliating to open them in public and shove the wretched things in. We walked to the train with our friends who came to say goodbye. As we were getting in we saw a small procession coming down the snowy path. First the Concierge with Connie's passport, second the Boots with her hot water bottle and finally the Liftman with a large empty suitcase found under her bed.

How much of this behaviour was intentional is hard to say. Given an occasion when she should look her best she would turn up in a miscellaneous collection of her nastiest clothes. Or if a party was on, she would vanish for the afternoon. She would harangue us all about how she should be running the gardens at a horticultural college with herself as head. She was at her worst with those closest to her, acting the Prima Donna until we were mentally pulp, then in a second be brilliant and charming to a stranger. People who went with her in her car were known to return by train muttering, "Never again!" Not that anything disastrous happened. Her driving should have terminated

Eric Booth holding his daughter Celia.

139

in the jug or the cemetery. Her Guardian Angel (she probably had a squadron on 24-hour call) was very much in charge.

"What can we do for her?" was the permanent question. Mother was right. "Never live with her, never worry about her. We have put her in God's hands and she will always come through." This was true. By now she had a flat on the coast with a companion-housekeeper. Even if this indispensible lady left, another would turn up. Connie would make sudden visits home and after a month or so, storm off to her own quarters. Later she bought a house, making a roomy flat from part of it, where she spent the rest of her life.

The next few years seem a jumble of events and non-events. In summer we had parties to organise and in the winter we had the business of closing down the house and re-opening it in the spring. We would go to milder resorts, sometimes Bournemouth, more often to Colwyn Bay in North Wales, when I would go to the nearest art school and draw. One year I was smitten with measles, an unpleasant

Celia Booth as a baby in Kenya.

thing to have when grown up, leaving me with ulcerated eyes and a long period when I was afflicted with boils. No wonder Job, who could take family tragedies with marvellous patience, was cast into near despair by the last!

After a very groggy summer we moved off to Wales again, this time taking a private house, not far from our Kenyan relations, and also Phyllis' dear sister, Violet, who lived in Bangor. Here we had the joy of a visit from Eric and Phyllis, with Celia, a bright little two-year-old and another baby due in the spring.

The visit began badly as Celia fell and broke her arm and also was found to be starting diphtheria, which, mercifully, she only had mildly. By spring time we were thinking seriously of buying a house in this part of Wales, but were dissuaded by Wyn who had seen a desirable house in the Lakes. We were back at Barton. Eric's family moved into rooms in St Annes, and Cicely arrived with Mary, now aged three. She kept us busy with whooping cough and seemed to be on the mend when Eric came over to Barton. He was sailing next day, leaving Phyl to follow in the autumn. He suggested that I should go with him, and Mother backed him up. So, making a dash to the shops to buy summer clothes and getting our local travel agent to promise to be at Victoria station, London, next day, with my ticket and passport, I left.

A great joy that winter had been making friends with Phyllis' family. They were Quakers who lived in Nottingham. William Armitage and his sister, Celia, lived in Jersey. He was a painter and his love of animals caused him to spend much of his youth following circuses and visiting zoos. His quick sketches were superb, better than the official portraits of prime Jersey cattle the proud owners commissioned, and along with watercolours, were the source of his income.

Aunt Celia had lived on the island of Pemba next to Zanzibar, running a Quaker mission with another brother. They found they must dissuade the Government from impetuously freeing the slaves, which they did by having them walk across the deck of a battleship and saying they had stepped on British territory. They felt the time was not ripe for such a move. The Arab owners were resentful, neglecting

Eric and Phyllis moved from Barton in Rumuruti to Kambi ya Swara near Nanyuki in September 1929.

Moving into Kambi ya Swara in 1929.

their old aged slaves whom they had used to treat as a member of the household.

Later Aunt Celia had run a Dr Barnardo's home in the East End of London, moving to another in Jersey, where she retired to a cottage in Gorey. This was a splendid place to go to in the coming years for holidays. To be there was a benison. Once she said to me, "The only temptations Our Lord did not face were those of old age. I therefore conclude that there is no such thing as old age." Very fragile, almost blind, she proved this, for one never thought of her as old, nor did she indulge in those hankerings for rest and comfort that so easily attack us. Later, to our sorrow, they died whilst the Island of Jersey was under German occupation. I am sure they endured their last years with peace and grace.

Meanwhile I was keeping house for Eric in Kenya until Phyllis returned with Celia and Phillipa Joan, the new member of the family. Later Cicely was back with Mary who had had a gruelling time, having developed mastoid trouble. I was staying with them when one day at breakfast a note came over from Eric telling us that the baby Phillipa had died, due to a most tragic mistake. I spent the day there with Celia and her nanny and the little white corpse while the distraught parents drove over to report her death to the authorities. That evening we buried her in the little coffin our Sikh fundi had made up in the hills above the farmstead. Eric as the father had to read the burial service as best he could.

Some weeks later I was due to go home. I had decided to fly. Imperial Airways had started a service two years previously, with that blessing, the Air Mail. The journey took only one week instead of the three or four when travelling by sea. I had never been in an aeroplane and might not get another chance. I think I was right in not taking a trial trip in the Wilson Airways, which our intrepid neighbour Flo' had started with the war ace, Campbell Black as pilot. I committed myself to the long trip and I should have to see it through. There could be no possibility of getting out, somewhere in the Sudan, saying I would prefer to walk - even if very probably I should want to.

First we went by train to Kisumu, sleeping at the hotel and in the

Phyllis and 16-month-old
Celia at Kambi ya Swara.

Celia Booth at 18 months playing music with her father Eric.

early morning rowing out to the seaplane on the lake. The take-off was really splendid. Roaring over the lake, the green water covered the portholes until we became airborne. Then we flew over the small islands, looking out for hippo until we came down at Entebbe for lunch. We gathered up more passengers, one being a Greta Garbo-like beauty, who had been photographing big game in the Mountains of the Moon.

One of the trials of flying in those days was that you were weighed along with your luggage. One really huge businessman had to cut it down to his briefcase and just about a razor and toothbrush. That night we slept in little thatched huts at Juba, a place swarming with the biggest and brightest fireflies. We landed as darkness fell and next morning waited on the Nile until the first streak of light showed where the horizon was. Once it was light we flew at 5000 feet looking at odd little mountains and dodging round clouds, which were having their own private thunderstorms, dropping a gay curtain of rain on the parched earth. Lunch was served in a tent by the river, a spartan meal of extremely dry bread, bully beef, stewed tea and tinned milk. I have a strong stomach but to be bounced about afterwards was too much.

The next night we slept at Malakal; here we picked up a District Commissioner's wife. The area under his care was as large as France and she said that nowadays there were so many people flying up and down the Nile that she was glad to be going to England to rest from entertaining them. It took courage to fly in a one-engined little plane. Next day we flew over the Sudd. This was a vast area of reeds and waterways, which from a height, looked like a large weedy pond, where the elephants strolled about like browny black beetles. The Sudd is roughly the size of Ireland. Some neighbours of ours, a General who took up flying when over 60, was forced down and was only found by the searching plane spotting his wife's white parasol. Even so, it took the rescue party three days to cut their way to them.

The next night we slept in a real hotel in Khartoum, luxurious after the others, but noisy as the lions in the zoo next door were in full chorus. Here we met the south-bound passengers who would use our comfortable flying-boat, while we went on in the four-engined

Hercules bi-plane. Amongst the passengers was King Albert of the Belgians on his way to the Congo, and Rudolf Mayer, the owner of the *East African Standard*. I asked Mr Mayer if he was enjoying the trip. It was, he said, extremely rough. "It is not often one has the privilege of flying with a King, still less a sick King," he added.

It really was a rough journey next day. The Hercules had been used for the first commercial flights from London to Paris and was a shaky affair furnished with cane chairs, which were not tethered to the deck. Whenever we passed over an outcrop of rock she would leap skittishly in the air, or avalanched us all to one end or other of the cabin. Our course lay across the Nubian desert following the railway built during the campaign to rescue General Gordon, and cutting across the great loop the Nile makes to the west. We knew that if we met a sandstorm we should have to land and sit it out, so when half way across we stopped to refuel at a spot known as Station Six, took off, circled round and landed again, we were resigned. It was no sandstorm this time but one of the engines which had packed up.

Imperial Airways refueling at Station Six in Sudan in 1932.

We sat in the shade of the wings whilst the pilot and crew clambered about what must have been the unbearably hot metal. This was real desert, flat unbroken sand as far as the horizon, the only feature being the railway line and the few flat-topped houses by the station. How the pilot landed so smoothly was a marvel. The only landing marks to show whether he was fifty or five feet above the white dazzle, were an old can or boot, which might be lying about. So we sat, becoming more and more parched, until we trailed to the station half a mile away. Here we were welcomed by a small very black Sudanese in charge of the place. He kept his temper, bless him, when some of us, who were very conscious of being VIPs, demanded instant rescue, if not by another plane, then by special train. They found it hard to accept that a train coming some hundreds of miles would cost a very large sum, so they must put up with some coaches a goods train travelling south would drop off in the early hours of the morning.

In the meanwhile this excellent man had an empty house swept out, got some chairs and a table and even string and wooden beds (at which they muttered, "Bugs!") and served up a stew made from his chickens and pigeons. It was good, and eked out our own rations of chocolate, sweet biscuits, tea and tinned milk. About two o'clock the promised coaches arrived and we roused ourselves to move into the most luxurious sleepers it has been my lot to use. Next day about noon the engine was said to be mended. Before leaving we all put money into a hat for a tip. Our black friend refused to take it, saying it was a privilege to give hospitality. Later I heard that an RAF plane made a forced landing there and the pilot and navigator emerging rather groggily from their plane, saw a black figure trotting across the sand to them with a cup of tea in each hand.

We flew to Aswan, staying in a hotel which had changed not a jot since it was furnished in the 1890s. Waking before dawn for our take-off at first light, we found a note from the pilot saying the plane was a write-off, so we would travel on to Cairo by the afternoon train. This was a wonderful bonus; we could visit the old dam, the Temple of Philae, and the quarries where those immense stones were cut. There was even a huge obelisk lying in its bed where it had been abandoned when it cracked just before completion. Also in the Souk there were many wonders, strangest of all – ladies' evening gowns belonging to fifty years back. They had boned bodices with leg-of-mutton sleeves, separate skirts with long trains, all made of cloth of gold!

The train journey was a delight. We watched a moving frieze of palms, camels, donkeys and peasants silhouetted against a sky, rose red and rising up to deep violet blue where the first stars shone.

Next morning our crazy journey reached another high peak of absurdity. There had been a slightly hysterical moment the night before when three subalterns from Khartoum had made an apple-pie bed in what they took to be the pilot's bunk, only to discover, too late, that it belonged to the Governor of Kenya's wife. Throughout all our mishaps she had managed to remain completely calm and immaculate. I know a lady should carry a pair of clean gloves in her bag, but she must have had at least half a dozen, while dust simply did not dare settle on her. On arrival at Cairo the red carpet was down and a crowd of grandees were there to meet her. The travel agent, busy sorting us out, remarked that she was down to spend a week there before catching the next plane. After a stunned silence the British lion roared, Lady B was going on, must go on to meet her son from Eton. Various red-faced generals blasted off, until the poor man was white and shaking. It was then the subalterns made amends by offering their seats to her and her lady-in-waiting. The agent promised them first class and all expenses on the next ship in gratitude. We were then whisked by seaplane, moored on the Nile, to Alexandria, an unusual concession, but appeasement was in full swing. All of this happened on the first of April!

From Alexandria we flew to Piraeus, almost touching the hilltops of Cyprus. Then we had a terrifying taxi drive up to Athens, and we were put up at the Hotel Grand Bretagne where, after all the heat, grit, not to mention the bully beef, it was bliss to have one's own bath in which to wallow, a long delicious meal and a marvellous bed.

Next day we flew to Brindisi. Being spring, the mountains were snow-capped and torrents rushed down their emerald flanks to a peacock-coloured sea. As Mussolini had forbidden flying over Italy, our cameras were put in a sealed bag on approaching the coast, and

*Young Celia feeding
the poultry at
Kambi ya Swara.*

we were in a train again, to travel to Paris with a short break in Milan. Then we flew to Croydon, the journey having taken eight days.

Before leaving England we had done a deal of house hunting. Owing to the Depression, there were many houses to view in the Windermere district. Most of them were built to face the view to the north, so that the bathroom and larder were the only rooms to get the maximum sunlight, or they were on so precipitous a slope that even the agile felt they needed ice axes and crampons to get round the gardens. At last, full of doubt, we looked over a Georgian house standing high above the ferry in the very spot Arthur Ransome puts Holly How in his delightful books. To our joy we found the kitchen wing had been pulled down and the whole place modernized. There was a billiard room where my parents could have their after dinner exercise and could step out onto a flat croquet lawn. All the lake lay below, and the terrace was rich with the scent of wallflowers and azaleas. Without

question this was perfect, and just as good the new lodge and garage where Dick and his wife could make their home.

After thirty years and unlimited storage we had collected an extraordinarily large amount of stuff. Fortunately, a hostel was being enlarged in Preston and needed to have furniture. Various charities and jumble sales did well, and at last it just came down to bonfires. It seems sad now so many old magazines and music belonging to the past just going up in smoke. It was hard to part with furniture belonging to the nursery, where the familiar sound of the brass handles in the vast oak wardrobe seemed a part of us. Still, we 'got shot' of it at last and moved to our new house where things settled down as if they knew they would be happy.

CHAPTER 11

Eric's Wife Dies and I Care for Celia

n September a wire came to say that Eric's wife Phyllis had died of typhoid, so there I was, flying out to Kenya again.

Celia was three years old by now, and we managed to get along somehow, though Eric was deeply shaken by the two tragedies. Nothing eventful happened until a day when he had gone to Nanyuki.

Eric and Joan in the living room of their house at Kambi ya Swara.
(Photo probably taken by Phyllis Booth).

Just before noon I noticed a cloud of smoke beyond our hilltops. Up there it was burnt out forest with thick bushy patches, and the wind was blowing towards us, where the best grazing lay. All hands were summoned and bidden to go and cope. I had a most uncomfortable feeling that they would not tackle the fire with enthusiasm unless someone was there to make encouraging noises - and that meant me.

I got into old slacks and my thickest soled shoes and started after them. It is curious how, on occasions like this, I find myself not advancing, but taking a crab-like scuttle to the side. Everything was tinder dry. The clumps of wild olive and laurel-like bushes went off like bombs, sending flames high in the air. Fire-fighting could only be done on the grassy patches, and you devoutly hoped the fire would not encircle you. I found the lads with long boughs of evergreen thrashing the grass in rather a lethargic way. Luckily the only Kikuyu words I knew were, "*Uka haha narua,*" meaning, "Come here quickly." This tickled them pink. "She speaks Kikuyu," they shouted, and plunged into action, stamping the large red embers out with their bare feet. We battled away struggling up and down the steep hills, coughing and blinded with tears. One ancient man had somehow got hold of a tin of green slimy water, and I envied them as they drank what appeared to be deadly poison to a European. It was exhausting, terrifying, yet

Part of a Kikuyu initiation ceremony being celebrated at Kambi ya Swara in the 1930s.

exhilarating. The end came at sunset and was sublime. We had thrashed away up a long grassy slope when on the ridge we met Hammis and his team of Turkana, fire-fighters. We had won. We collapsed gasping for air. Colour, tribe, sex did not exist. We were down and out and triumphant.

Mercifully Eric turned up in his ramshackle old car so we could all pile in and be driven the five miles home. I know I drank two glasses of water and seven large cups of tea, non-stop. My feet were tender for a week after, but we had saved two thousand acres of good grass, most desperately precious at that time when the country was enduring five long years of locust invasion. These hatch, if conditions are suitable, far away in Somalia. For six weeks they travel on the ground and are fairly vulnerable. Then they take to the wing. According to the wind they invade Arabia, even India, more rarely coming south. Now with insecticides sprayed from the air, and with the co-operation of the countries at risk, they can be controlled. When locusts visited Kenya in the 1930s there was no locust control; they brought bankruptcy, famine and suicide.

It is said eight locusts weigh an ounce, but when they settle on trees at night, like snow they break off the boughs with their weight. I have seen knee-high grass eaten down to brown evil-smelling stubble, in a couple of hours. Everyone was ordered to carry a home-made locust swatting stick, not that it did any good, nor did dashing about the garden banging saucepans, though it did help to let off steam. The biggest swarm we saw from high ground, we reckoned to be fifteen miles long. Driving through it we clocked up four miles and visibility was almost nil. That was only one of many swarms. They gradually weakened. Great flocks of kites and storks and baboons followed them, and I think every religion prayed for deliverance. One friend said, "I wouldn't mind them so such if they didn't wear that cynical smile on their faces."

One day Eric developed a high fever, as did our cook. There was a doctor now in Nanyuki, a man who had got into a matrimonial mess in England, and whose mind, I think, had been affected by the publicity and strain. Anyway, having collected him in the evening,

The cattle dip at Kambi ya Swara.

he pronounced both patients to be suffering from undulant fever. It would immediately subside after the injections he would give next day, he said.

By this time it was late so I offered to put him up. His great fear was of leaving his lady-love alone so he insisted he should return. It was not much fun driving the extra 30 miles through buffalo-infested forest, with a tricky ford and some shaky bridges, knowing the journey must be made next day again. He gave the injections and most fortunately took blood samples. He was very optimistic, but a few hours later Eric's temperature was 106° and the cook looked ghastly. Jack had come over and we stuck Eric in the tin bath and sponged him down. I rather think I collected the doctor again as he wired for a nurse to come up from Nairobi, another complication, as the railhead was at Karatina, 50 miles away. Afterwards he said he had quite overlooked the fact that there was another nurse in the district who had left her case that very day. Later the one from Nairobi turned up. She was a difficult person. Born in Africa, she was sure we could not cope, yet grumbled loudly at all the usual upcountry drawbacks, disliking our coffee and refusing our tea. I did feel sorry that our neighbour's donkeys came over and fought ours with the ferocity of bulldogs, and very much more noise.

A day or two later the Doctor taxied out to say the results of the slides had come back from Nairobi. Eric had malaria and Cook had enteric. Their fevers were down to 103° and Jack insisted they both go to Nyeri, where there was a small nursing home and an African hospital 20 miles further on. This was wise for Eric was naturally feeling very low and sure that he would join the graves on the hillside.

We got hold of a lorry and fixed him up on a mattress, while I went ahead in the car with Cook and an elderly carpenter to keep him company, as well as the doctor. Jack had insisted that he should see Eric safely installed, but I must say I found the journey a trial. First, through being in a state of fuss, I took the ford too fast and got water in the engine and stuck mid-stream. The lorry driver remarked that he knew nothing about cars, so Eric rose from his bed and gave directions, which got the car going again, but only just. Every furlong or so it would splutter and stop. Then the doctor put on what I can only think was his maternity manner. Patting me comfortingly on the knee he would say, "Keep it up, little woman, you are doing splendidly." We travelled until sunset when we had a puncture. There was a farm a short distance away, but no one was there and I felt very stuck. Just then a car full of men going up to what was hoped would be a goldfield, arrived. They mended the wheel, got the engine cleared of water, and took the doctor, protesting that he ought to see his patient, back to Nanyuki. The lorry had passed us and was miles ahead, so we put the doctor in the Nanyuki-bound car.

The nursing home was said to be excellent at inducing the quick birth of babies, and no wonder. It lay on the far side of a valley and was reached by bounding from one boulder to another and then crawling up a very steep slope. This had not harmed Eric, in fact he had cheered up a bit, safe in bed in charge of a competent Scots doctor and motherly nurse. We pushed on to the grand new hospital beyond Nyeri. After explaining slowly and carefully Cook's case history to the Indian sub-assistant, all I could get was, "Oh, but I cannot admit. He has no temperature." Saying he jolly well had to be admitted, I fled back to the White Rhino, the little hotel in Nyeri, getting into bed about midnight. Next morning Eric was very much better. The first of the new anti-malarial drugs had just reached the country and he was responding well. Greatly cheered, I went back to the White Rhino (someone had made the joke, quite unfairly, that it was so named because it charged on sight), had lunch, and was having a well-earned siesta when a loud, "Hodi," and bang on the door got me up. It was Cook who, beaming with joy, announced, "The Daktari says I have no fever and I am well. I am going to eat two sheep." Neither police officer nor Commissioner seemed to know what to do with this highly infectious man, who was likely to die if he took solid food. I really couldn't blame him for hating the big clinically clean wards of the hospital. He was used to the comfort of a blanket by the fire in a hut with the company of friends and livestock. Then I remembered there was a famous Scottish Mission at a place called Tumu Tumu, which happened to be Cook's own part of the world. We went there and, Glory Hallelujah, they took him in. He was entirely satisfied and recovered.

The thorns of Africa are several inches long and needle sharp. They have a way of working through the tyres, acting unitedly in very much the same way as ants when brushed off a branch will wait until some hundreds are in position before giving the command to bite. That weekend I had at least six punctures. With such major mercies about, they were only a minor irritation. My travelling had not finished yet, as I had to return to the farm and take Nurse to the railhead. Once there, to our joy, we found a train pointing in the right

The view of Mt Kenya seen from Kambi ya Swara.

direction. Nurse now said she must travel first class. It was her right. The Indian stationmaster was appalled. No one had ever travelled first class. It was going to be done now. The poor man wrung his hands and looked to heaven. Long, long ago the first class key had been lost. It must be found, she insisted, and so a search was started, whilst the train stood patiently in the station and the African passengers, not bothered by time, extracted great entertainment from the scene. After much rootling in drawers and cupboards amidst clouds of dust, the key was run to earth and the First Class compartment opened. The stationmaster was quite right. I do not think anyone had used that carriage since the railway was built. Festooned with cobwebs, thick with dust and possibly housing all manner of creepy beasties, it looked like a Haunted Room in a rather bad film. But Nurse was happy, sitting in lonely grandeur, and with all those shiny clean second-class carriages empty, the train moved off and I waved her a fervent goodbye.

A few weeks later Eric and I went on a convalescent trip to Durban and back in a tubby little British India ship. On board were two schoolboys, the third generation of an Indian family to go to Harrow, along with their aunt, a delightful lady who was the leading woman doctor in India. They were bound for Johannesburg where the boys' father was Consul. I can hardly bear to write it, but there were white-skinned passengers who nicknamed her Mrs Ghandi (not by way of an honour) and also protested that they had the use of the first class dining saloon! I must add that this was the first, and the last, time I met this attitude, but I still feel sick with shame.

Late in the spring, Celia, Eric and I sailed in a German ship. Clean and very efficient; people were packed into her like sardines. Celia and I shared a cabin six foot square and no porthole, with a Swedish-American missionary and her three small children. So she and I got into the habit of sleeping on the fore-hatch where we could watch Orion swinging above us.

Her Captain sat in the saloon after dinner, and would bring out a tartan-covered book of comic Scotch stories. He would stand and read this in his very Germanic voice, then saying, "For'zee benefit off our Cherman frients, I will now translate," which he did, telling us that the tight-fisted Aberdonian could be substituted by an East Prussian, who was always good for a laugh. On the last night, instead of his joke book, he told us that enormously long story, probably invented by the ancient Greeks or even earlier in history, in which somebody returning home has the news of his father's death broken to him by a long rigamarole beginning with trouble with the mice.

One day news got round that an order had come through that the Swastika flag must now be flown. This, I thought, might be a slightly historical event. So I went on deck to be the only spectator. A glum petty officer ran the flag up, and some half dozen sailors gave a feeble salute, (not the fascist one), and with no heel clicking. A bugler stood by, and as he seemed doubtful what call he should sound, did nothing.

That night one of the passengers went overboard. At the end of the voyage at the gala dance someone lined his place at table with purple flowers.

In the Mediterranean we hit rough weather. Coming on deck I was told I had missed some magnificent seas and a man suggested we go to the weather side where we might see something. We saw it all

Joan Booth back in England in the 1930s.

right. A solid wall of green advanced towards us. "This is it," I thought, as it picked me up most gently, carried me along, putting me down in the scuppers unbruised and soaked to the skin.

We landed in Southampton joining the Armitage family in a lovely country house hotel near Barnstaple. Here, quite suddenly, I had what I suppose was delayed reaction to the last few years. I could not sleep at all, eating was difficult and concentration impossible. I spent one night trying to memorise the 23rd Psalm to no avail, and strangely, I still cannot repeat it. I just trudged about, and after seeing a young doctor who gave me no help, I returned to Belfield with Eric. Here our doctor gave me what I think must have been luminal, whereupon I became drunk and giggly, being apt to go to sleep at the dining table.

Eric returned to his farm in Kenya in the autumn. Celia lived with us at Belfield for the next four years. She went to a day school and joined companionably with the many children in the district and her cousins.

Cicely came in 1934 with Mary, now seven years old, and an enormous baby on its way, which the doctor only diagnosed to be

*John and Ada Booth
in the Ladies' Garden
at Barton in 1929
before they moved to
Windermere.*

twins when they were arriving. Father, Mother, Mary and Celia with 'Micky' McClellan had moved up to our beloved Shap Wells. Cicely had Nurse Greenwood to see her through the birth and the next two months were so packed with crises that we felt quite peculiar when we had an event-free week. Matthew arrived promptly, but Susan not until four hours later. Then Cicely became infected by what for years had been ignored as a grumbling appendix. The nearest hospital was in Kendal and it was thought inadvisable to move her there. This meant we must strip and scrub my bedroom so that a great man could come and use it as an operating theatre.

Within twenty-four hours Cicely's sallow face had turned pink and more healthy than it had looked for years. Poor Matthew was returning his feeds with the velocity of a soda-water syphon, gaining no weight and visibly withering away. Good Nurse tackled our doctor and another specialist came from Manchester, diagnosed it to be pyloric stenosis and took him back that evening to be operated on the next day. It was on a Sunday evening and the old Rector bustled in with a medicine bottle of very grubby water, which he said was

John and Ada Booth's home Belfield in Windermere where Joan also lived, and where Celia was brought after the death of her mother, Phyllis.

the stuff from the River Jordan, and christened both babies in the best china slop bowl. Then baby was raced to Manchester. In all the summer traffic they somehow got there in time for the operation to be successful.

Meanwhile Susan developed curious blue patches. We took her for observation when we went to collect Matthew and mercifully her heart valves, or whatever was the cause of it, adjusted themselves on their own. Matron in Manchester said that Matt was splendid, but a more pitiful mite I have never seen - he was still only five pounds in weight and his hands were all a-quiver. It was then that we had our drama-free-week and felt odd. Soon the family were home again. I said to my Mother that it was splendid that she had taken it all so calmly. "You do after the first four," she replied.

Cicely and her children went back to Kenya in the autumn of 1934, when the twins were large and fit, coming back again in 1937 when they were three years old.

CHAPTER 12

I Join the Oxford Group

n September 1934 my mother told me that the Oxford Group, which she had been reading about a good deal in the *Spectator*, were to hold a small House Party in a hotel near Kendal. It seemed it was an upspringing of a new, or renewed, spirit amongst people of all denominations or none. Mother wished she was well enough to have gone to it.

Thinking these people might be able to help poor unhappy Connie, I suggested to her that we went. Connie was reluctant, saying she would rather go to Morecambe to look up a new friend; after a while she agreed to see what they were like. She would go in her own car so she could leave when she wished. Cicely, who was at home, looked at me, and said, "Perhaps you will be the one to get caught," which I felt was insulting.

We set off. After a few miles Connie overtook me and careered ahead. At that I felt positively homicidal. She was, I thought, breaking her word, and if she passed the hotel gates I would catch up with her and ditch her car, even if it killed us both. I was wrong; she turned in at the gates, stayed a few hours and then, bored with it all, left for her seaside flat.

I stayed watching and listening. It was a very mixed bunch: couple called Sanderson, mill-owners from Galashiels, who were now living in a cottage in order to keep their work-people employed; an Oxford don, delightfully witty and famous for his learning; a young farmer from the Border; and a score or so others from all walks of life. They had something in common. With no earnest effort they had a peaceful radiancy, a kind of unshakable inner joy and purpose in life. A purpose to change the world's problems, in the belief that human nature can be changed. This started with themselves and was possible - only possible - by the miracle of God's Spirit and direction. This shining quality I could see in my parents, although their goodness did not have the aim to bring about a spiritual revolution. It was a quality for which I hungered. It was simple, practical and mostly costly. Only when I faced myself – my greedy, lazy self, with all my antipathies and long buried hate – in the presence of the absolute holiness of God, His love, His honesty, His purity and self-giving, only then could I lay my defences down and let His new life come in. The absolute part was quite appalling, but it had to be that if there were to be no excuses, side-stepping or self-protection.

Somebody gave me a bit of paper and pencil, suggesting I write these four absolute qualities down and then ask God to speak to me. The one blazing thought that came was that I must commit myself to Him. Going down on my knees, I asked Him to reveal Himself and show me the way.

I talked to a woman and told her of the burden of trying to be nice to my sister Connie. I said it was very like a boxer retreating into his corner before facing the next round of bashing. How utterly tired of it I was, yet I felt a Judas because I could not give her an honest kiss. "You don't love her with the love of Christ," this woman said.

At home that evening I wept because I knew I must write to Connie, this terrifying woman, asking pardon for the weary past. Then came the compulsion to add, "And from now on things will be different." It seemed mad – the biggest gamble of my life.

Then there was Sandy. We had never written love letters, but I was hugging an uncontrollable physical hankering. It must stop, I must write and tell him what I was taking on and there would be no more letters from me. I was very much afraid he would scoff.

Next morning I found myself whistling and singing about the house. A thing I had not done for years.

Connie's reaction was prompt. She rang up saying she was coming back. Curiously enough, for the first time in years all the beds in the house were in use, save one in my room. Normally I would have said my nerves would not stand sharing a room with Connie and listening to a list of the faults of the family and society – 'Russian Tragedy' was our name for it – so this really was a test.

When I saw her coming into the hall I saw a most pitiful woman who needed a great deal of loving and found myself giving her a hug and kiss. It was not me at all. It was not the old me when I lay quite unruffled whilst she talked through the night. This must be what St Paul called being 'transformed by the renewing of ones mind.'

Sandy's letter followed soon after. There was no mockery, but real understanding with a note of envy. I had thought that in doing what I felt I must I should have to black him out of my mind altogether, but strangely I could think of him and pray for him without a touch of the old pain.

Also, I found I could look at a photograph of the little baby, who had died, without emotion. I simply could not bring myself to look at it before that. Eric came into it too. I had flown out to be with him and comfort him in his sorrow and achieved so very little. Now in reply to a letter I wrote he said there must have been some infection in mine as it had roused him to drive 200 miles to see one of these Oxford Group chaps. He had a really honest talk with him and had committed all he knew of himself to God and so found peace of heart and joy.

On the last evening of the House Party there was a very special meeting and I was urged to be there. However, it was perfectly clear to me that I must spend it sitting in the drawing room reading St Luke's Gospel, as if for the first time in my life. To read an account of Jesus, a historical character who, to people's surprise, "spoke with authority." How silly that I should cringe at reading the Bible in the drawing room! Somehow it is not a thing one does. "Joan's got religion," might be said. Well, what if she had? I sat down in an empty room with no interruption. I read carefully and slowly. When I got to the bit where Jesus asked what was the use of gaining the whole world if you lose your real self, something crashed open. Almighty God, Who orders the immensity of the Milky Way and the intricate dance of electrons and molecules, is seriously and lovingly concerned about each petty little human being. He had gone to the utmost length of suffering to break the barrier of our self-willed sin, and this out of pure love.

It was then that the statue stepped off its pedestal and became more alive and nearer than anything in His creation.

A very minor product of these days was that I had lost my spectacles. I had worn them for some years in a vain attempt to ease the bad headaches I had every ten days or so. Not wishing to miss the meetings, I took the chance of driving the car without them. After three weeks – and still no headaches – it seemed they both had gone.

Next Sunday I dutifully went to Communion in that semi-reluctant fearful state as before, to make the discovery that it was all true and joyful. The Bounty of God pours out in love as we give our petty selves to Him. This wonder had flowed over me like music over a stone-deaf person. Instruction, earnest effort, all so very worthy and burdensome, went. What I had never attempted was the one thing needful – to make an experiment of trust and obedience. I'd put the cart before the horse, painting, decorating, oiling the cart, while never considering the matter of traction!

I began to write, and found my spelling improved, in itself a minor miracle. Also, having opted out of teaching in Sunday School, I now knew I should. I went to the Rector and told him that if he was short-handed I would be happy to help. He looked at me in wild surprise, if such a prosy old gentleman could be wild, saying that I was the first person ever, in his experience, to volunteer for the job. For ten years I cut my Sunday pudding to dash down to the village for what I found to be tremendously satisfying fun. Fun to be able to use drawing, music and story-telling. Not so much fun when, instead of a Bible story, it seemed more effective to share with them the fears and messier bits of life; somehow it is costly to own up to human faults in oneself. The reward was the, "Oo, do you feel like that?" as the child realises we are all very much alike, and can all find the same help.

Then there was singing. I had a good voice but was so self-conscious that it could be a misery. Infuriating too, when other people who I thought did not sing so well tackled second rate stuff with the utmost aplomb. I became very serious, deciding I must sing to the Glory of God. The next time I went on a platform I forgot all this glory business but saw a crowd of very pleasant people and was delighted to have songs lovely to sing. I hope they enjoyed it; I know I did.

About this time Celia was ill with a very high temperature. I got into a rare old state of panic until I faced the situation in absolute honesty. She might die, or get better, or have a long illness. In all these possibilities God was in control. So on my knees I deliberately took my worry off the child. At that moment she sat up, gave a loud mixture of a cough and sneeze, cuddled down and went to sleep. Should I sit up? No. I went to bed to wake in the morning to find a perfectly restored child. Had my worry acted like a blanket of smog preventing healing coming through?

Joan and her niece
Celia at Gorey, Jersey
on the water front
below Gorey Castle.

These early days of belonging to a small group had their comic times. We used to meet weekly and felt that it was not for mutual improvement but having begun this adventure of a new life, we must pass on this Good News.

Not knowing where to start, we left it for a week. One of our number then had a letter from his native village near Barrow-in-Furness, saying that some of them had heard about the Oxford Group and would be glad if he would come and tell them more. Well, that was the answer to our question. We were ready, if a bit anxious about going, and quite appalled when, on our acceptance of the invitation, we got a poster back. It announced our visit very much as if we were a *pierrot troupe* giving our names and wildly incorrect descriptions of who we were. We hurled it on the fire, and set out feeling that a greener, less experienced bunch of people could not be found in England. On arrival we found Ivan Menzies of the D'Oyly Carte Opera Company and son of the local doctor, fairly dancing with rage. He had been working with a group in the East End of London and had the strong compulsion to go home that weekend. Our frightful poster was the first thing he saw. It only took a minute to straighten that out and we started our campaign with a friendly, and very talented, native in our company.

Some months before I had been holding forth vehemently about something when a friend very cattily said, "I can just see you in a Methodist pulpit!" That Saturday night I was actually in one! Also like us all I had a horror lest anyone should ask me if I was saved. During refreshments afterwards a jolly old party bounced up to me crying, "I can see you are saved. Shake hands." Well, I hope I am.

That Sunday at evensong the big parish church was packed with the usual congregation, the various chapel folk, and plenty of lads of the village who had come to hear Ivan who had been a bit of a lad himself. The service was taken by the nice old parson in his typically parsonic voice. As he continued, his voice changed entirely into that of a genuine humble man. At the end of the set service he turned and said he would hand over the rest to Ivan, and he, with all his gift of wit and drama, somehow sanctified, spoke. Ivan ended by asking all of us who wanted to take this road of faith and guidance to stand up, and many church and chapel folk stood.

It takes time for a middle-aged, middle-classed spinster to learn to widen her horizons. To let the world walk through her heart and to deal with small things, those small hinges on which bigger things hang.

It was about this time our cook had to leave us and the kitchen maid took over. Irene was young, intelligent and had a flair for cooking, but was very rough in word and deed. She was the daughter of a Cumbrian coal-miner who had to go down a thousand feet, then walk half a mile, climbing some hundred steps under the sea bed before reaching the coal face. He took tea cakes for his bait as they packed up smaller in his stomach when working doubled up. I liked Irene but I felt that the conventional thing to do was to give her a Talk for her Good. Oh dear! Memories of school pi-jaws! What a mercy that I had learnt to sit quietly with pencil and paper and let Someone wiser direct the stream of thought in my mind.

"Have you ever thought what you owe the coal-mining community?" was the first thing I wrote down and soon I was telling Irene how I had woken up to the debt we owed, and the admiration for their toughness, courage and fellowship amongst her people and how we all needed to learn to be like that. The climate altered considerably. She still would throw fish scraps into the little courtyard for the cats to worry, but the revolutionary thought came to me not to tick her off, but get the biggest plant pot I could find, fill it with geraniums and put it opposite the scullery window. This was a complete cure, and no word said.

Life was not easy, nor will be. A challenge came that winter. There was a large gathering in Malvern. I went for a week. People were there from all over Europe. From early morning until evening there was much talk, study and times for quiet, with plenty of fun and great dedication.

All through it was the theme of working together as a Team. No lone wolfing, but a united body. From the moment I had gone to my first large party, still more at school, I had detested teams. Our little bunch of friends in the Lake District was comfortable, but this was huge and horribly disturbing. I ceased to sleep, my mind whirled like a clockwork toy lifted from the floor. At last I left and after driving a few miles I was aware that I was bursting with joy. I was leaving that team business behind. Let the world go hang, I was not going to be involved in it.

Then I passed someone. I did not see his face, only the tall lean figure with red-gold hair, a long drab raincoat, and a carpenter's bag slung on his shoulder. In my heart I felt it was Christ on the road, with broken boots, with the unemployed and hungry. It was a few minutes before I pulled up. To go back and identify myself with this 'team' idea was sheer agony. But it was inevitable. I turned around, but curiously enough, I did not see the figure again. At Malvern I ran into a sensible woman to whom I could talk the whole thing over. We had a few minutes' quiet and both had the thought that the week's stay was enough and I should go home. I had learnt my lesson. Reaching home, I straightway ran into a friend with a deep-seated hatred of her father. She wanted to talk about it and make the decision to hand it over to God. In doing so He lifted the hate out of her life.

CHAPTER 13

Eric Remarries and Celia Returns to Kenya

n 1935 my Father and Mother celebrated their Golden Wedding. Our doctor was quite worried at the idea of a large gathering of relations, and all the jollifications we were bound to have. She said one or two people seen quietly in the drawing room was as much as Mother could stand. Far from it! My Mother spent the days going out and receiving hordes of people. In fact, on the third night, she and Father went to a dinner party, whilst I went to bed early with a drink of hot milk and brandy. There were numerous presents, the best being a bound album with the names of all the employees. All the money they received they gave to charity.

Next year King George V died, and, more personally for us, we received the news that Eric had re-married. My Mother felt strongly that Celia should go out to join him and get to know her step-mother. I made enquiries and heard of a girl with whom Celia could travel to Kenya. She lived in Fishguard, which I thought would be a most difficult place to get to, after the London, Midland and Scottish Railway (LMS), stated they knew nothing about trains running on the Great Western line. It was November and foggy weather for driving, so I was delighted to hear there was a simpler way to get there. You went to Liverpool, changed stations and boarded a boat train, which took you there. I set off. At Liverpool I saw my train moving out of the station and was urged to pursue it by taxi to a little station on the outskirts of the city. No luck! I had missed it again! The stationmaster advised me to take the next train to Chester, where I should get something going my way. It was growing dark and the fog was thick. On Chester station a little band of Wales-bound travellers wandered from platform to platform on the advice of that strange voice from above which haunts stations and can so seldom be understood. Eventually we got into a train, which crawled along through Shrewsbury and into South Wales, becoming emptier, while the guard would come from time to time to ask, "Are you the lady for Fishguard?" in an awed kind of voice.

At two o'clock the train stopped at Swansea, with me as the sole survivor. The stationmaster, a most sympathetic man, took me to the waiting room, and rightly said it was no place in which to spend the night. He took me into his office, where I sat, feeling almost royal as he telephoned for an engine to shunt the carriages in some siding into the station where the morning train for Fishguard would leave, and warm it up. This done, he plastered a carriage with 'Ladies Only' labels, dug out a couple of blankets and a pillow. "Better turn the slip inside out," he said. "We don't know who used it last?" (This was the very best bit of the saga, as Celia said when I got home, which it was).

Next morning in glorious sunlight we chugged past banks of flowering gorse down to the blue sea. At the Fishguard station hotel I had a bath and a huge breakfast, before spending half an hour with Miss Thomas, to see if she would be a suitable person to accompany Celia back to Kenya. Satisfied with the interview, I boarded the train and finished the day at Preston at midnight, where I found a hotel. Since then I have never wanted to travel by the Siberian Railway, but I have the highest regard for the South Welsh and that stationmaster.

We packed Celia's things and I went up with her to London, staying along with her Armitage relations at a small hotel where we could meet Miss Thomas. It was the night of the Abdication, and we heard Edward VIII make his speech in that agonisingly strained voice. Leaving the room a minute later I found the hall porter, a leathery old soldier with a double row of medal ribbons on his coat.

171

He was weeping, saying over and over, "He's let us down." Now it is an historical event to be read about in books and people seem to have forgotten what a family thing it was. Just after the abdication a very John Bullish man said to me with great indignation, that an American had asked him how we British were taking the event? I am sure it was done in all friendliness, and that the poor man was both surprised and affronted when the Englishman blasted off at him in fury. I knew that he had been unable to explain that it was not the time to discuss the hurt and awful disgrace when a beloved member, as the old soldier had known, let the family down. It really was a very black hour. Then we saw a delicate, ultra-shy man pick up the enormous load and through the darkest hours of our history make a triumph of his short life.

Another thing I should like to set down is that people look back with disgust at the appeasement that went on when Mussolini and Hitler were behaving like rampant madmen. I would ask them to try to remember that the carnage of the First World War was still with us as if it had happened the other day. You could not have gone through those years without the reaction of, "No! Not again." It only came home to me when passing through a large hotel lounge I saw a bunch of army officers talking together in a corner. The sight was like a heavy physical blow. I felt sick. I could not have believed it, but that little glimpse as from the past, had that effect. I am sure everyone else was raw inside, although we didn't speak of it. It affected our thinking and policy.

At home I went through another longer spell of strain. Night after night I would take a sleeping pill with my hot drink and fall asleep, only to jerk wide awake ten minutes later and lie rigid with my mind whirling. I found going through the Litany helped. The words are beautiful. It reaches out to other people's need and is a protection from self-pity. There came a night when my depression was so bad that I decided to own up. I was at the bottom, bankrupt in every way.

With overwhelming clarity the answer flowed over my mind. You are part of my jigsaw puzzle. It matters not a jot that you do not know the completed picture. For whether you are a bit of dim background or vivid foreground, each piece is essential to the whole pattern. That started a long slow crawl back to health and ease of mind. I have had illnesses, both physical and nervous, since then, but I hold fast to that truth. Only God knows how much 'use' one is, and it is a constant battle not to fuss, to be driven by people's opinion or sink into apathy, pretending that laziness or cowardice is humility.

I can't think why there is that false streak in us which makes us say, "I am a rabbit," when asked to play tennis, and feel that diffidence is a lady-like quality. It's deadly, I mean Deadly, leaving life wide open for the Bumptious Bullies to get going. Once at a big family gathering a friend said she needed a birthday card drawn for a special person. I kept quiet, thinking, "Oh no, not me." Later I took myself to task. I wanted to apologise in private but was constrained to say, "I'm sorry," in front of everybody. "Oh, good," said my friend. "We need another card to take a welcoming poem for an engaged couple." The, "Oh, no," immediately welled up, and with a gulp I managed to say, "Oh, yes." Now the extraordinary thing was that instantaneously I had a clear picture of that card, including how to draw the prancing carthorse, which should take up the bottom left corner. It was great fun drawing it too.

Cicely came home from Kenya with her family in 1937. Jack was having Meniere's Disease of the middle ear, a grim thing for such a fine horseman. Their twins, Matt and Sue, looked like flies, which have been picked out of the milk, after their voyage. They soon picked up and when snow came in November, they chirped up like little robins. They were entirely different in mind and body, so could be up to double the amount of mischief one small child can play.

There was a lot for me to learn. Matt could generally be depended upon to be sensible when on walks, as he was already deeply committed to cars. One day he went wild, as all young things do, and cavorted ahead, crossing the road on a bend. Because I was scared I lost my temper and shouted at him that he was very silly and naughty (which he knew). I gave him a really vicious slap. He looked up at this towering furious aunt, and knowing he could not do what he would like to do, picked up a large stick and bashed his dear Sue who cried, "Don't do that Old Man."

It was that autumn that Mother died after a long series of heart attacks. She had a wonderful month when she said she was, "on the crest of the wave," and after a happy evening, listening to Gracie Fields at her funniest, she went to bed, and was hit in the early hours of the morning. I hope that after the first minute or two, she knew no more distress. Father handed her over to God's keeping with wonderful selflessness, and indeed, though he missed her sorely, the freedom from constant anxiety and broken nights, caused him to improve in health. We all felt it was a mercy that she was spared the pain of saying Goodbye to the McDonoghs when, with war looming large on the horizon, they headed back to Kenya and there was little chance of her seeing them again in this world.

After they sailed and with Celia gone, the place seemed very desolate. One of the things which hurt was the silly fact that there was no need to leap over toys and bricks scattered on the floor. In spite of all the reasoning I could muster, I found I was swamped in an uncontrollable unhappiness. I was grateful I could go up to Galashiels and have a real honest talk about it all. Bena did not tick me off for being weak and emotional, bless her, but welcomed me with affection unsmeared by pity. I remember her saying: one gives to the young but must not expect, still less demand, gratitude, for love is their right and must be free to grow. It is a fact difficult to accept. As for getting over a deep-seated misery, I hope I am learning that the process has nothing to do with effort. That only produces the feeling one is bashing one's head against a wall. Even if every bit of you cries, "I can't," you have to relinquish it at the one place where Christ relinquished his life. That is where God, who is no vague Goodness, and who understands our weakness, abides and brings healing.

By this time we were being advised how to make gas-proof rooms, a task, which seemed impossible. Also we were buying material for black-out curtains and painting over skylights. It was a debatable point whether windows should be squared off with gummed paper, some people arguing that glass blew in, others that it was sucked out. A neighbor, who was high up in the medical world, was busy getting Jewish doctors out of Germany. It was still possible to swap a brilliant specialist, or surgeon, for a prize bull or stallion! We were urged to be 'Grim and Gay,' but I think we felt more exasperated or just cross.

A couple of years before I had gone with a friend to a meeting in Exeter where a young German explained the philosophy of his country. He said how gladly all Saxon-descended people in Holland and Britain would join in a glorious German state. Somebody mildly remarked that perhaps such countries would prefer to preserve their identity. The German seemed bewildered at this, "But, of course, they would be glad to unite," he said. It was strange that we merely thought, "What a chump," and did not hear the alarm bell ringing. By now we were facing the grim possibility that the war would start with a huge air-raid of poison-gas-filled bombs. Thank God there was none of this and when the blitz did come there was much neighbourliness and gaiety.

The Women's Voluntary Service (WVS) and the Women's Institutes got into action to cope with the organisation of evacuating women with babies and children into safe areas. Most people seemed unable to understand that townsfolk would find no charm in the peaceful countryside, and possibly be unable to understand the local dialect. Our district was crammed with large houses in which rich and elderly couples lived in great comfort, so it was a pity our local Council sent out a billeting officer with instructions to make it plain that they were forced to take in some horrifyingly large number of children or else face prosecution.

Two villages where the reception of refugees was a relative success were where the billeting officers – in both cases women – went to great pains to stress the nobility of taking children in, the wisdom of putting the mountains of bric-a-brac away, and helping people to realise that even 'dear little girls' can be just as, if not more, destructive than boys, when bewildered and resentful.

Perhaps it was because Father welcomed our officer with friendliness and a glass of sherry that we were blessed with three dear children, Ted, Ken and Dolly Ritson, from Newcastle-upon-Tyne. During the 'phoney war' their mother pined for five-year-old Dolly and took her home, so we had our number made up by Brian Ritchie and later, at the request of them all, Eldon Hardy, who wasn't happy with his 'billet wife.' This was the name those Geordies invented for their hostesses.

We were blessed at that time with a very dear cook. Margaret was most intelligent, lively and enormous. When her father, a famous fell runner, came back from the First World War her very trying mother retired to bed with strong hypochondria, leaving Margaret, aged twelve, to run the house and bring up her four little brothers. "The little one was only two so I had to take him to school with me, where he was so good sitting by me." But she added, "They do say that if a child calls you mummy when you are young, you'll never have one for your own." Well, she married her dear Allan who would bicycle twenty miles of an evening to woo her, and has two splendid sons, which gives the lie to that superstition. She certainly knew how to manage boys – with affection and unruffled calm. Once she found Ted weeping in the coal shed because he had an irresistible desire to punch Brian's head. His mum had sternly forbidden such behaviour. Margaret agreed with him that Brian, though well behaved, was so dreadfully dim and smug, that she often longed to punch him, so, Queensbury rules being kept, he had better go and do it.

He did, to the great benefit of everybody. Eldon, on the other hand, did not need punching. He was one of a huge family, very small and wizened, with bright, blue, eyes and a small permanently red nose. He told us, with great pride, that he helped his Dad look after large cart horses, and I am sure he would do, though should the beast lift its head Eldon would have swung at least two feet off the ground. They tried to speak an English we could understand, but kept the delightful lilt in their voices. The only thing which got us puzzled was their vowels – "Mi friend Porcy went to chorch in mi short," did sound odd. It was lovely to have children in the house again and reserve a time in the evenings when we could read adventure stories, or play games, while Ted was initiated into billiards by Father.

Before they arrived we had to go to the parish hall where a retired doctor lectured us on the effects and treatment (if any) of poisoned gas. All quite sickening, and delivered in an artificial jolly voice, he described severe nerve pain, mental disturbance and death.

Then there were the days when we fitted everyone with gas masks, except for the babies in arms, whose elaborate enveloping bags had as yet not been issued. It was the middle-aged ex-service men, who knew what gas meant, who were the most harrowing as they tried to cheer us up by making jokes.

Being a small county, Westmoreland dealt with much clerical work on the voluntary system, such as petrol rationing cards and food rationing. A large room filled with middle-aged people at school desks toiled away, getting some fun when an application form stated the applicant's employment was 'an invalid' and even 'a Baronet.' I was glad to find that we all muttered the alphabet to ourselves when indexing names, a habit you feel is a private weakness.

It is hard to believe, but in one Cumberland town the boys from a Newcastle Grammar School were herded into the town square and their potential hosts walked round choosing which they would have. "That's a strong lad, he could help carry the coals," or "Not that one, he's spotty."

"Like the Babylonian slave market," one boy said, with marvellous good humour. How frightful it must have been to be the last one left.

The first of September was the night when the blackout came into force. This did not only apply to buildings and street lamps, but cars were forbidden to use their head lamps and the parking lamps had to be dimmed by fixing a piece of tissue paper inside the glass. Should an air raid alert be on then even these dim little glimmers were switched off. They did not help much to light the road but did, one hoped, prevent cars colliding. Westmoreland roads are all very twisty, generally bounded by dry-stone walls and with jutting rocks and trees to add to their picturesqueness. This was a good thing as no-one but a lunatic would drive at any speed even before the blackout, and now even they crawled along. The Council were busy employing men to paint three white bands round the trunks of trees and also the projecting rocks. This was a great help; in fact, I cannot remember a collision during that time. This convinces me that if roads were made to look dangerous they would be far safer. Our drive was tricky at the best of times, overhung with trees and going down into a little dell and then climbing steeply to the house.

A cousin from Camberley with her two little boys and a martinet of a Nanny was staying with us. The elder boy and I had an enjoyable time with white paint making all these hazards safe. I don't think he had ever had the chance to slosh paint onto large stones and trees, nor had I, for that matter, so we found it most satisfying.

The trainful of children from Newcastle-Upon-Tyne and South Shields arrived on September 1st. Sitting in the car waiting for them I wrote some very bad poetry. It is rough and raw; but that is how we felt.

> Hush now, my soul; go very humbly
> For you have known
> What all the easy years successively
> Have never shown.
> For you have seen Christ walking hell again
> Lonely and bright.
> The pretty things have gone. A flame
> Of strong compassion flares across the night.
> The furtive cars crawl down the dusky ways
> As pain stalks in the soul. The Idiot Fiend
> Tears the poor bird, the Holy Dove and it has seemed
> No further horror can be thought on, or lies heard.
> Bow when the heart is breaking
> Our bowed heads dip
> To drink this bitter cup of our own making
> Pressed to our lip.
> When we accept the load of guilt that's piled
> against the soul's light feather,
> We turn to help the child,
> Who soon may be a mangled lump
> Its bright life split and flung upon the dump
> Of the world's rubbish. There together
> With Carthage, Rome and that Jerusalem
> That knows not peace.
> While still the Timeless One walks on. The Friend
> The terrible I AM.
> How can we cry then that this is the end? This must cease?

Which are the transient things that shall endure
The dragging years of selfishness? The moment pure?
These are the ageless. These poor moths
That flicker in the fire.
The uprooted weeds that hooves have trod
Down into pulp. It shall transpire
Because these folk knew pity, learnt to love,
Have shown compassion,
Obeyed the Will within them. In their fashion
Looked upon death and laughed, and prove
They are of all Eternity. Their home is God.

All the same, delivering the children to their billets was no easy matter. "I am ashamed of my class," said a forthright, well-to-do Australian friend, and indeed one often was. On the other hand an elderly brother and sister, who boggled for half an hour before taking in, very reluctantly, a pair of siblings, made a wonderful home for them and a rich friendship lasting long after the war and even to the end of their lives. By eleven o'clock at night I was driving round, having failed at four houses, to get a small boy a bed. In the Council estate I stopped to ask the way. The woman said, "Can't ye find a home for lile lad? Well now, let him come to me. Ah've gotten fower, and another won't be any trouble. Coom in luv."

Two homes were taken over by the Council; one for a hospital for those children who had impetigo and scabies, the other to give them temporary accommodation, should their hosts be ill, away, or busy with relations home on leave. A number of us would go to these homes to cook and clean. The cooking was hard work as the kitchen was fitted with an immense Eagle range; black cast iron and steel, it devoured coal like an old-fashioned railway engine. Stoking and heaving huge pans were good exercise. It cured an attack of lumbago for me in one day. I had hobbled into the kitchen wondering however I should manage, and decided at dinner time that intense heat and exercise had not been as pleasant as deep rays and massage, but had had the same effect.

CHAPTER 14

War Years in England

n 1942 Father slipped away from us. Our doctor warned us that he had an obstruction. As he was well in his eighties it was his opinion it would be wrong to put him to the alarm and pain of an operation, done possibly in a much bombed town. He was in duty bound to tell us and get our consent. My brothers most rightly thought the same, and Father did not know he was ill. He was finding the war puzzling, more than distressing. Not that he was senile, but his reactions were slow. Then in September he took to his bed saying it was a very long time to wait for his next birthday, and a sad disappointment that the Preston Guild was to be postponed until we had dealt with Hitler. He could remember the guild of 1862 and had hoped to attend five guilds in his life, which would have been quite an achievement.

However, he was very cheerful and kept saying, "I have had so many blessings," and one afternoon he just died, with barely a sigh. It was the week of our harvest festival and, as his funeral was on the Monday, the church was a mass of glorious flowers, fruit and corn. This seemed absolutely right. He had had a fruitful life and was safely gathered in. The only time I wept was a few nights later when we had an air raid warning. The tears were of thankfulness that the dear old man was not going to be alarmed, hurt or bothered.

We stayed on at Belfield for a year, Connie and I. The staff had left so I got down to the work of cooking, and had, before father's death, the five fires to lay and light each morning. Fortunately I am one of those who enjoys cleaning a grate and getting a good fire going. In fact it is a permanent temptation not to meddle with a fire, especially if it is in someone else's house and not going well. Eldon and Brian found new billets and the Ritsons decided they would have their sons back at home, so there was a very tearful farewell to be said to them.

As usual when closing a house there was a tremendous amount of sorting to be done. Father wished each of his managers to have a painting or some token, which disposed of plenty of the big oil paintings and some silver. The quite enormous picture by Mclease of the death of King Robert of Sicily took up the whole of one wall and was crammed full of priests, monks, men at arms grieving, relatives scheming and villainous uncles, as well as the poor old King and a smattering of choirboys. The Preston Art Gallery accepted the painting, where no doubt it still moulders.

On Ken's suggestion our much loved Old Master, an Ecce Homo said to be by Caracci, went to the Garstang Church, which needed something to warm up its very austere Georgian interior. Connie and I could pick out the furniture we should need when the time came to set up house and the other bits were divided. We set out a lot of glass and china on the billiard table for the family to choose. Amongst them was a glass dessert set from the Kenyons. As Wyn looked at them I heard him murmur to himself, "No, I'm being sentimental and greedy," and he passed them by. The next day I found a list of how my mother would have liked things divided and it was a joy to see she wanted him and Ken to have the set.

We did some entertaining. Because Lancashire was so much engaged in various forms of war work, refugees were not allowed to stay in the county. As a result, Westmoreland was packed with them, as well as with schools from all over the south. These refugees, almost all elderly Jews, lived frugally in whatever rooms they could find. They appreciated spending an afternoon in a private house. Being city dwellers they did not notice the garden, but over coffee and cigarettes packed themselves into a room where somebody would play Viennese music, and so make a tiny Middle-Europe. One said, "We hope by now all our relatives are dead," a remark which brought home to me what was going on more appallingly than anything else.

Amongst the people staying in our safe area was an elderly English spinster. She was a caricature of that type, with wispy hair crowned with a hat, which looked well sat on, cotton gloves and gentle vague face. Nothing much could have ever happened to the likes of her, I thought. Not a bit of it. She had been a governess in Berlin. When the Great War began she was unable to leave. "I was shot at once or twice, but fortunately I was not hit. The worst experience was when the mob went for me. The police got me into their station in time. After two hours they said they could not keep me any longer. The crowd was waiting for me, but as I went through the door an officer who had been called to interview me, stood on the step. As I passed him he clicked his heels and gave me a beautiful salute. So I walked through the crowd unhurt."

During this year I had gone on with my bed making and cooking at the hostels and added a two-hour watch locked in the Air Raid Precautions (ARP) room with some half dozen telephones. A most complicated list gave instructions concerning who should be rung up in case of an Air Raid Alert (yellow), Raid (red), All Clear (green). What happened if these warnings overlapped was never revealed, which was a blessing as we never had a daylight alarm. The only event during my spell of duty was a wonderfully gossipy message in the broadest Westmoreland dialect from a country Bobby about a plane crash. I passed the message on in modern English. On my next watch I found a stiffish note saying that messages must be taken down verbatim. I still wonder what would have been said had I written: "Weel now, it's like this? Lile lad 'as joost coom in an' 'e sez there's been a plane crashed on t'fell, etc." All of us who took this job on found it delightful. To be locked away from interruption for two whole hours was a rare luxury, and I had a poor opinion of one house-proud friend who took her silver to clean, when there was time in which to read and write. By chance there was a bookcase there where I found Jane Austin. I am ashamed to own I had never read her, solely because my elders advised me to do so. I also discovered Trollope. In those days many people found themselves turning back to these wholesome solid authors, though I never got down to George Elliot or Charlotte M Yonge.

One nephew went into the Air Force, training in the USA, while the other joined the Navy, so the brothers coped with the firm, which was no light job. We employed twenty girls doing nothing but sorting and counting food coupons and filling forms. Many things need not have been rationed if it was not that even high principled people developed a strong sporting instinct to get all they could lay their hands on. One old General, I am sure the soul of honour, boasted that in his travels reviewing the Home Guard, he had collected six pots of marmalade - looking on this as if he had got a good bag of woodcock. What shook me was that the most unlikely people would say, "Of course, rations don't apply to you," which made me want to give them a sock on the jaw. Telling Wyn about this, he sympathised and said he found the best reply was that he liked honesty, and being in the position where he had to sack people for dishonesty felt he should practise the former.

What has been untold is how the older men faced the war years, or how many small businesses closed because their owners had died of overwork. These men, whose health had been undermined by the First World War, now shouldered extra work due to depleted staff and rationing, on top of which they did ARP duty and were out with the Home Guard. Many of them dropped in their tracks.

The choice before me now was to be called up and sent to work at Short's flying boat factory on Windermere, or look round for some whole-time employment more in my line. Fortunately, the couple who were in charge of the children's hostel wished to leave, so I offered my services. It seemed better not to work on a voluntary basis. The Committee would not then be in the embarrassing position, as they were with an elderly woman who had taken on the commissariat of the two houses, so I was paid £1 a week, which meant they could sack me if they felt they should, instead of having to be grateful. The food was truly dreadful. Unpleasant soup and cottage pie were served on alternate days for the main meal, for weeks on end. Gathering up all my courage I would go to see Mrs C, determined to be reasonable and polite, but we always ended up in a fish-wife yelling match. This would result in vastly improved menus for a few weeks. What made me hopping mad was that special delicious little dishes would arrive for me, often of liver or something equally good for children. However, it never took long before we reverted to the soup-cottage pie routine. She was unable to grasp that large schoolboys, who had been playing football or careering over the fells with the Home Guard, needed more than bread and margarine. "I have it myself," she would say.

When things became very tense we would have highly comic sessions. The Chairman, the same old party who was so jolly about poisoned gas, always began by saying what a great pleasure it was to talk things over in this friendly fashion, while the rest of us glowered. Of course, I should have had the courage to threaten them with my resignation, as they would have found it difficult to find someone to take my place. Mercifully, she left and was replaced by a sensible woman who fed us better. The last years were made happier as we had visits from an inspector who provided comfortable chairs, and even toys. It had been pronounced that evacuees would certainly destroy these, so they were withheld. We demonstrated that this was not so when I dug out two gay bedspreads to use as tablecloths. They kept the first spotless for a fortnight and were delighted when it was I who made the first spill.

After a long tussle with the Committee, they allowed us to use the big Esse stove and found it more economical to run than the one gas ring, on which we were supposed to cook breakfast and supper. Being an institution, our rations were helped by tins of apple jelly made by the women of British Columbia and parcels of tinned soup. Then the children of Akron, in the States, sent boxes of unbelievable delights from the ten-cent stores – pencils, rubbers, pretty handkerchiefs and beads – we had not seen such things for years. Marvellous they were for prizes, or Christmas and birthdays.

What I found hard to take were those people who said, "Aren't you lucky," to the children. No child could say, "No," and would have been looked at with horror if they had. "Lucky, my foot," I'm sure they thought, "with Dad at the front and Mum being bombed and yourself in a strange land, where you could not understand people's language or ways." They responded if you said things were pretty horrible but we all had a go of making the best of it.

One summer holiday lasted six weeks when it rained as it can in Westmoreland. We rigged up a kind of Punch and Judy tent from clothes horses and sheets. I had read that fun could be had from puppets and made some comic types from felt and odd bits of cotton. They were a smash hit. Moreover, cocky children behaved normally because they were not seen, and the bashful ones became chirpy for the same reason. Most touching of all was to see a rather withdrawn child sitting in a corner having a really good heart to heart talk with the little man on his hand, who wagged his head in a truly understanding way.

I wish I could tell stories of how I gave a vision of the future and a living faith to those children. But it was I who did the learning. One night (and with double summer time, it was light until eleven o'clock) we had been driven mad by two rampageous little girls. I then suggested we were quiet and let God speak to us. They looked uncomfortable but swore they'd had no thoughts. I could honestly say the thought that had come into my head was that I should stop nagging, trust them and go downstairs. The rest was silence.

Also there was a grammar school boy who came frequently. Very stunted in growth, everybody called him Goliath. It suddenly occurred to me one morning that he might not like this; but it took two hours of polishing a floor before I swallowed my pride, and could say to him, when he came in, that I was sorry I had used his nickname, and would change to his proper name if he wished. Instantaneously his face changed from stubborn mulishness to that of a cheerful boy who said, "Oh, that's quite all right."

Our two most lovable and trying children were a red-haired, sapphire-eyed Irish lass and a small boy called Tony. It was interesting that they both had a leg in an iron. This gave them, it seemed, terrific pugnacity and they never, never gave in. At the end of a long day's fighting and yelling they would be flat on the floor, still shouting defiance and able to give a shrewd kick with their iron. Often one had to carry them upstairs and get them, somehow, into bed. Then they would sleep for fourteen hours or more. I wish I had kept in touch and would like to know what happened to them.

Then there were Dennis and Brian from Barrow-in-Furness, living in what was, according to the billeting officer, a lovely place. This was a handsome Georgian house in the country, where they lived in the kitchen. I guessed it was dismal, and knew they were not allowed to play in the garden, but must go for walks with the housekeeper. Dennis lived in a world of impossible dreams. "I was chased by a mad bull," he said, on coming indoors. He always disobeyed any order or request, expecting to be clouted when he came in at the door, and was physically the most beautiful human being I think I have seen, with a bloom of health on his lovely skin. When I said he hadn't much hope of being a skipper or an Air Force pilot if he didn't do what was expected of him, his reply was that, by then he would be in Borstal.

His friend Brian was a much more reasonable chap. When it was time to go back to their billet, he got into the car, whilst Brian fought the whole way from under his bed to the car door. That afternoon I had a telephone message that they had gone missing and next morning, at seven, two very damp, tired boys were at my back door. They had walked the 16 miles back! They stayed quite a while, while I battled with the authorities for a better place. At last a really good hostel with its own farm took them in. Brian dived under his bed again. Dennis tried to cheer him up, saying he knew the place, and they even had a bull there. "Ah've seen a bull," came back the tearful voice, and we had to frog-march him to the car again. They did settle there all right and I constantly find them coming into my prayers. The wise old, Quaker gentleman who took them to Heversham said, "You know, you are what you think you are," a remark I have pondered over a lot.

Then there was another Irish child. Mary was a beauty; she would crawl into one's lap for a bit of comfort, and crawled into your heart for sure, but her billet wife had thrown her out and the officer said, "She had a bad name in the village." That was quite an achievement at the age of four. The bad name made it difficult to get her placed. Eventually a home was found and I went with her to it. A nice woman, I thought, with a kindly voice. Across the road was her old billet, where a tired slattern yelled and slapped her half dozen of a family.

It did give you an insight into human nature and I frequently decided we were all barmy, myself included.

The barmiest event during the Barrow-in-Furness blitz was when children were taken, by coach, to Appleby, at least 70 twisty miles. There, those who had infested heads, were bundled into the coach and sent to our hostel, at a guess another 50 miles. They arrived at about nine o'clock at night and I was instructed to rub them well with paraffin and tie their heads up in bits of old sheeting.

Some W.V.S. gave a hand but first we had somehow to find them hot drinks and bread and margarine, that being all we could lay our hands on. As there were only 18 beds in the house and most of them full, they had to sleep on the floor. They were too tired to care and slept like logs. Luckily the next day it was blazing hot, as there were endless head washings. Our old chairman arrived on the scene to inspect them and if one nit was found the head had to be washed again, though I am sure the creatures were dead from exhaustion by then. It was really hard on those little girls who, in spite of the blitz, had arrived with their hair waved, even tinted - so golden, glossy and artificial they looked.

We were blessed in being only five minutes walk from open moorland. There were rocks and heather and those tiny tinkling becks where you can build dams or send the little boats you make from rushes, on adventurous voyages. A perfect playground, and a place where on one's two hours 'off' you could go and, resting your eyes on the encircling hills, regain a bit of sanity.

Our great joy was the Westmoreland Festival of Music held every other year in the spring. Being the mother of all such festivals, it had a very high standard and could call on the Great to adjudicate and conduct. All the villages sang like conscientious competitive larks at the competition pieces (there were no solos), and the Big Work. It kept us busy all winter and in May the little town of Kendal was packed with old friends and rivals. One glorious time before the war, our village of Bowness, trained by Nancy Bowness herself, carried off all the prizes.

During the war we had the good fortune of having Dr Armstrong

Gibbs, notable composer and choirmaster, living in Windermere and coaching us. The peak of glory was that black winter of 1941 when it was a real struggle to get together and sing. Everyone was sick of those daily maps in the paper, showing the horrible fat arrows of the Nazi advance. I know that summer I had got into a sleepless frenzy, saying, "Oh the poor Dutch – Norwegians," and so on, until I realised with a jolt, that what I was really fearing was the time when those arrows got so near it would be a case of, "Oh, poor me!" Shame filled me so much, I leaped out of bed and knelt, saying, "I am a vile coward and utterly self-concerned." After that it was all right; I could pity without fear.

Nowadays we speak of that time as if we were all as lion-hearted as Winston Churchill. I knew I wasn't. But that is a digression, for there we were in the spring of 1941 singing the Messiah under the baton of Sir Malcolm Sargent. We sang with the glorious confidence you have when led by a supreme master of his craft, who was illuminated by his faith. It had been a long exhausting day. Even so we all felt, "If only we could do it again because we are at the very gate of Heaven."

CHAPTER 15

My Work with the Oxford Group

The war came to its end and the evacuees went home. There was a great deal of tidying up and then I was free. It seemed right I should make my home in Preston, for I owe all my comfort to industrial Lancashire, let alone the very deep loyalty one feels to ones own native town.

It was at this time that the McDonoghs left Kenya and bought a farm in Natal. Standing on a station platform in South Africa Cicely felt a hand on her shoulders. "Wheer d'you coom from?" asked a voice.

"From up the line," she said.

"But wheer do you coom from."

"Same as thee," she answered.

"Aye, Poor Proud Preston," said the old porter. Goodness knows how he had discovered this, but word does get round.

Cicely's daughter Mary came over to study music in London, and soon after Celia followed to take a secretarial course, followed by a job on a large farm. Meanwhile, I had found a house on Bank Parade of all places. I asked a young architect to vet it and he said he thought it could be turned into a ground floor flat with a maisonette above for the amount of money allowed for restoring buildings. It turned out to be riddled with dry rot. The compensation was the large living room, with its two windows looking south at the famous view.

At that time there was much talk about the housing shortage. I had a young couple living on the ground floor, but it did seem that one woman ought to share a house with three bedrooms. I began to make enquiries whether there was another single woman who would care to join me. Names cropped up only to come to no conclusion. So in my rather skimpy prayers I owned my plan was not working, and I would stop bothering, leaving God to take control. The next morning a friend in Blackburn rang to say she was being sent to Liverpool at short notice to run a club, so the young couple staying with her would be homeless. I felt that the Almighty was calling my bluff, but after my discussion I could not say no. Jim was just out of the RAF and taking a Diploma of Education and Sally, one of an enormous Roman Catholic family from east Lancashire, was convalescing after a miscarriage. I did not guess that I was being given a son and daughter, and eventually four grandchildren, as dear as if they were my own flesh and blood, with the incalculable joys, sorrows and fun of a family.

I had got to know a parson and his wife in Blackburn, They had four children and had been stationed at Tien Tsing, where he was chaplain. Returning just before the Japanese entered the war, they had left a social life with a large house and wonderful Chinese servants, for life in a large stone vicarage, where the cellar was always full of water, standing on a bleak hill overlooking a forest of factory chimneys. Monica, witty and brilliant at anything she took up, was constantly smitten with migraine. Even then she would twist a battered old hat into a new shape and sally out to make a happy instructive evening for the parishioners. Johnny was quiet, with a neat wit, bad eyesight and deaf-aid. He owned it was a blessing to be able to switch this off when his small sons at the 'gang' age stampeded through the house with their friends.

I went there for a weekend when the girls were getting over scarlet fever and stayed six months, as the boys then caught whooping cough. I now know what life is like in a vicarage with callers at back and front doors, telephone going and small boys vomiting in the kitchen. Being used to large families was a great advantage. Those years of austerity, so annoying because things should have been getting better, not worse, were easier in a large household. One egg a week, two ounces of margarine and pound of meat for one person, work out quite well when there are seven in the house.

There were other families wanting a helping hand, proving that an odd-job woman or aunt is a much-needed person in the community. I went two or three times to a young couple living in north Lancashire. The first time was for the birth of their baby. They were in rooms in an old farmhouse, where water had to be drawn from a well, or the water-butt, and boiled on the sitting room fire. The privy was down the orchard where an immense carthorse would frequently stand before the door and was quite a job to move.

I spent the first few nights with the husband's parents who lived in a beautiful seventeenth century house down the road. It was here I experienced the nearest thing I have known to a ghost.

When shown to my room I involuntarily said, "Oh, how lovely," This was odd as it was far from beautiful. The old door closed with a latch and there was a fine stone mullioned window. Everything else was shabbily Edwardian, but a wave of peaceful happiness washed over me and caused me to exclaim. That night I went to bed and was soon asleep. Then I woke to hear the latch move and the door open. I am used to the oddities of old houses, so I only thought briefly, "Bother, need I get up?" before snuggling down. In a few minutes the door closed and the latch clicked into place. The next night I woke knowing something was going on, but I did not know what. Then a very heavy weight seemed to be dragged over the end of the bed. Slightly frightened but not panic stricken, I said a short prayer. I did not speak about this until a fortnight later, when having coffee with Mrs Baker. She asked if I had noticed any thing in that room. She said her son in the Navy refused flatly to use it. On the other hand the dogs who are usually sensitive to atmosphere, showed no fear. Several times her Daily had come in with two cups of coffee because she had heard someone walking above and presumed one of the sons was on leave. "I can only think," Mrs Baker said, "that in times of persecution, of the Risings, someone found sanctuary there and left an impression behind." I think so too.

Several times I went to that beautiful house in Cheshire. Irene Prestwich of Tirley Garth had lived there with her parents and a huge staff, including 16 gardeners. When her parents died, rather than move into a small house she offered it to those of us who were working for Moral Rearmament. This was the name Dr Frank Buchman had forged for the Oxford Group in those years when all the world was re-arming. He had foreseen that without spiritual and moral strength the coming war could not bring victory over evil.

Throughout the war there were very many people passing through London, or staying to work at printing and sending out news. Most of their time was spent in cellars under blitz conditions. Irene's offer was accepted, and soon the place was transformed. Eight girls turned the lawns and flowerbeds into a market garden, providing food for the house and the people of Liverpool. Other men and women came to keep the big house in its old beauty and order whilst swarms passed through. You might catch a bishop and a private soldier scrubbing the kitchen floor together, and getting great benefit from the spiritual and physical exercise or a bunch of coal miners or school teachers taking a rare day off to think for the days ahead.

The place has grown vastly ever since and the whole world seems to drop in. Those early days were not easy, even for Irene's generous nature. She said she found giving up her orderly quiet home most costly, still more the gardens her father had created. Now they are back in their old loveliness and many hundreds visit them on Open Days and her dream that people should find more than beauty there has come true.

Once I had a message from London to say there was a great shortage of cooks at a large hotel at Caux in Switzerland. Wrecked by refugees, it had been bought and restored by the Swiss to be a centre on neutral ground where the nations could find healing after the war. When I got to London I heard the need had been met. The shortage now was in the basement kitchen in Berkeley square. All kitchens are places where one can give a hand, so for a month I worked there. I stayed with friends in Barnet. Being a country mouse I found the 7.45 gallop by underground, and foot, quite exhausting. It astounded me that the Prescotts found it relaxing. The day generally ended about nine in the evening and was so full there was not time to write letters. Also there was a heat wave on. At the end of the month I returned, secretly feeling rather noble and certainly tired, to be met on all sides with: "How well you look after all that lovely Swiss air."

CHAPTER 16

Switzerland

and South Africa

got to Caux the next summer, It was a very rich time. Just as in Tirley and in London I worked with an international team. Many were Scandinavian and there were two Finns, whose language is different from any other in Europe, save Turkish. Our work was to do the flowers and in that big place this took the whole day, going flat out. It went without strain, though at the end of the day our legs were apt to buckle under us. It proved that if we started the day with a short time of quiet, then shared what we felt should be done, and also tidied up misunderstandings (it's very easy for us women to be either bossy, or what's worse, keep quiet and then feel hard done to!), then the work went smoothly and happily. I had learned, when cooking at Tirley, that it was necessary to keep on telling myself that people are more important than things. In that vast kitchen there could be half a dozen people making cakes, cutting sandwiches and so on. There was the overwhelming desire, which every cook knows, to shout, "Get out of our kitchen and let me get on with my job!" It was a real discipline not to do so, and strangely if you managed to think of the people around you, dinner would be on time.

Far more than our little bit of co-operation in running the place was the privilege to meet people from all over the world. There was a stately Imam and also a Buddhist Abbot who spoke from the platform one morning, saying that the simple but drastic truths found in the New Testament were in their own holy writ, and that on these fundamentals we could unite and work together.

Back at home, we came to realise the Bank Parade house was crumbling about us. It was sad to leave just when we had changed the jungle into a garden, but in 1951 a pleasant house came up for sale. It stood opposite that of my nephew who was newly married, in a pleasant leafy road across the river, and we moved into it.

The Preston Guild should have been held in 1942. Now there was a thirty-year gap, and austerity had got us all down in the dumps, so people talked of letting the whole thing lapse. Only one woman Alderman and a Labour Councillor had held office in 1922, the time of the last Guild, and they fought bravely to keep the tradition alive.

People did not want a local millionaire to be mayor. It is a great honour but exhausting and expensive, so there was an impasse. Then a dentist and his wife volunteered to stand, providing that politics did not come into it. Slowly people began to paint their shop fronts whereupon their neighbours did likewise. The little back streets were fettled up with sham flowers and bunting, goodness knows how. Although clothes were rationed, somehow pageants and superb processions were devised with the ardour the North puts into its Walks. Brass bands came out and banners, as well as cohorts of little girls in white frocks and baskets of flowers. There was a real Cardinal with his Knights of Malta about him. Agricultural and industrial shows filled the parks. People put their chairs on the pavement and would call, "Sit down, luv. You're looking fagged." The loyal Prestonians returned from the ends of the earth and the Freemen enrolled their sons. The Mayor and Mayoress played their part nobly getting cheer after cheer from the crowd in the market square on the closing night.

The year before, Celia had returned to Kenya and become engaged to a coffee planter's son, Hugh Owles, who was managing a farm north of Rumuruti. They were married in February 1952, a week after the death of King George VI.

Queen Elizabeth II spent the night of her father's death up in the

Tree Tops Hotel in Kenya watching big game. A pleasant little lodge had been built for her in the forest. The Governor was turning a blind eye on the stirrings for freedom, which were soon to turn into what was called the Emergency. Residents formed a guard about the Lodge and six women made it pretty with local wild flowers. When the new Queen returned there for luncheon, the news of the King's death was broken to her. It had been arranged for a car to take her to Nairobi and from there she would fly to Entebbe, where a large plane would take her to England. The Queen gave orders that the car should wait until she had written six letters of thanks to the women who had made her house so charming.

Celia's aunt from her mother's side, Violet Armitage, and I had planned to visit Kenya. Violet had heard so much of our life there and longed to see the places her Aunt had worked in the 1890s. So we booked a passage on a Dutch ship leaving Southampton on December 3rd for a leisurely cruise round Africa. We would see the Canary Islands and the Cape. No one seemed to think the unrest in Kenya would come to much, so with great delight we boarded the *Klipfontein*.

It was the first day of that famous 'smog' which lasted for weeks, killing many people, and making the country come to its senses about the necessity for smoke abatement. Our last afternoon in England made us thankful we were heading for the sun, for it was intensely cold. The train bringing passengers from London was held up by fog and arrived hours late. On board we met many elderly Dutch people who were escaping the winter too. We were quite overawed by the comfort of our large cabin and private bathroom. As for the first meal, we gasped at the huge menu – one page full of Dutch dishes, the other English. We had not the capacity to stomach what was considered a normal meal, though after a week or so we adapted ourselves, even to the famous East Indian Rice Toffle.

Within 24 hours we were in warmer airs and by the time we reached the Canaries it was hot. The quayside was busy with people selling large walking and talking dolls, and the shops in the steep main street were of wonders. Splendidly built women strode up and down the streets with big loads on their heads. They wore those straw sailor

The Klipfontein in Tenerife in December 1952 headed for Africa.

hats the Navy had used and we wore as children. I wondered if they had copied the Navy, or did the Navy acquire them a century before? In Nelson's time the matelots wore varnished boaters, but they were part of the Navy's rig in the 1840s. There is a delightful cartoon in Punch of Queen Victoria, Albert and the children on board the Royal Yacht, dancing the hornpipe and wearing them.

As we sailed south I found my wonderful evening dress – the first for many years and made from this new-fangled stuff called nylon – acted like a portable Turkish bath when it touched the deck. I had been able to make a set of underclothes without using precious coupons, as we could buy war stock parachutes. The one I got (I think it cost 15/-) was of real silk. I still have some of the yards and yards of rope. When it is unravelled it is perfect for button holes, and is precious because of association and also quite unbuyable.

Cape Town was an entirely new Africa for me. What jarred me even more than seats reserved for blacks or whites, was the very first thing I saw; a large muscular deck hand walking along the quay with his lunch, which was a wrapped white loaf. I had heard that, in the post-war elections, the Nats had promised to scrap the wartime bread, which was wholemeal and restore white bread.

We had three days in Cape Town then made for Port Elizabeth and celebrated Christmas rounding the Cape. After a day in East London we reached Durban where we put in for six days. We travelled up to

Pietermaritzburg by couch, where Cicely was living The twins were just finishing their schooling and they were planning to sail to England soon – Matthew to study engineering and Sue, nursing. Matt spent some of his holidays on farms as Afrikaans is a compulsory subject in exams, and coming from Kenya he was handicapped in knowing none.

CHAPTER 17

Our Ship Sinks

Our next port was Lorenco Marques where we had to admit the Portuguese know a lot more about suitable architecture for the tropics, as well as the elegance of carrying a pretty parasol. Here we were loaded with copper up to the Plimsoll line, and then sailed on for Beira. Those of us who had been down the coast of Africa before were puzzled that we were so far in shore, barely two miles out to sea. Beira is a small port, and there were two ships astern. The mistake of trying to cut comers to secure a berth was proved when, during lunch, there was a long shuddering scrunch, with the feeling that tins were being opened under us, which was more or less what was happening. All the crockery fell to the deck with a crash and the *Klipfontein* stopped with a nasty lurch. The mothers made a dash for the children's playroom. Mercifully, the ship did not roll and go down like a stone, which she could well have done, but very slowly the list began to increase.

The Purser came into the saloon and said we had better get some things together and go to our boat stations. Vi and I had quantities of family things in our luggage. I had my mother's silver hand mirror and she had lace and embroidery, lovely bits and pieces her clever fingers could transform. I am sorry I did not pack a suitcase with these treasures as well as clothes. I could have done, but I was feeling distinctly queasy with panic, sharks being in my mind. Stern duty, which often enlarges unnecessarily upon the Voice of God, seemed to insist that I take the minimum of things, which would be useful in an open boat.

The Klipfontein hit a reef near Beira
on 8 January 1953 at 1:20 pm and sank at 4 pm.

On deck we waited for the lifeboats to be lowered and it was a help to have some children in our party to help with their life jackets and so keep busy. The boats came down with difficulty. Ropes and derricks had been painted a beautiful snowy white so that they stuck, descending with jerks. Astern one sailor fell into the sea when a rope broke, but was fished out. This meant those people allotted to her had to be squashed into other boats and leave their bits and pieces behind. Otherwise there were no accidents, but it was very unpleasant being lowered, and worse trying to cast off, hammering away at the paint whilst the boat bashed the ship's side. It seems odd that seven years after a war when so much shipping sank, the ship had this trouble. Just a few days before we had been shown all the wonderful radar and depth-sounding equipment and thought how safe we were, but the smart lick of paint was almost our undoing.

Once away we wallowed mightily and were thankful it was not really rough, and the day was overcast. It might have been the wallowing or a kind sailor passing round a large box of Black Magic chocolates, or perhaps sheer fright, but I became sea-sick for the first time in my life. For years after, though owning them to be excellent chocolates, I could not bear the smell of them! When the episode was over a splendid old colonel started on about "brave little women" and I replied, "Brave be blowed, I was sick with fright," to which he replied, "So was I."

I found I could not watch the *Klipfontein* take her final plunge. We had grown fond of her and I didn't want to view the nasty sight.

After that a dhow came bowling along manned by bronzed men in scarlet loincloths. They offered us a tow, which we declined. By now we could see the smoke of the *Bloemfontein Castle* on the horizon, so they left to gather what flotsam they could and we waited a couple of hours. When the Bloemfontein came, she lowered her lifeboats. These came down smoothly, being worked by motors. One was left attached to the ship, whilst others towed us to it. Then there was the rather tricky scramble from ours to the other, which rose up to deck level. We were shown into the lounge and tea and coffee and whiskey were served, to warm us up.

This ship was putting in time between returning to Britain, making a Christmas cruise up to Beira and back. A few cabins were empty and we tried to be thankful for them, horridly claustrophobic and below the waterline as they were. The next morning we were asked to gather in the smoke room where our captain made a very embarrassing speech. He had been a light-hearted young man on his first all round Africa run, and seemed to spend a lot of time chatting up the younger passengers. Now he was swamped with self-pity. We had lost things, but he would probably lose his master's ticket. We heard later that he got off very lightly.

Afterwards a steward came in with an armful of clothes, which he placed upon the deck, saying: "There's been a whip-round for you ladies, so help yourselves." I was glad to find a nightdress. There was also a nylon dress made to fit a tall thin woman, so I handed it to an American from Boston, or maybe Cape Cod, where people are said to be even more aloof. She had been very sticky during our trip, but now she was transformed. She would write to the *Times*, she said, to tell of the wonderful generosity of these gifts. Good heavens, didn't she remember what the States had done for us all through the war years, and all this gratitude for one cheap frock!

The fact is that this very mild disaster acted as a kind of judgement day, which is what disasters are for, maybe. Somehow people divided into those who got steadily nicer – and those who did not. There were those who were grateful for the very good treatment we were given. Our 'bar books' were refunded, as well as £50 spending money, and everything was done to get us to our destinations by sea or air. Those other people were determined to squeeze every penny from the shipping line and talked about taking legal action. One pretty widow, who had superb clothes, and who bought arms-full of presents at each port for her daughter and the grandchildren she had not yet seen, wailed that it was pointless now to visit them. She seemed unable to accept the idea that a live Grannie, who had had adventures, was better than things.

We landed at Beira that afternoon. Sitting on the steps of the Immigration Office, we filled in two large sheets of most complicated questions about our forebears, voyage, age and lots more, the whole lot ending with the question, "Can you write?"

We dispersed here, most of us being transferred to an Italian motor ship. Luxurious and air conditioned so as to be chilly below decks, she travelled so very fast that the vibration of her motors made everything creak and nearly bounced us out of our bunks. Sadly, she ignored all those smaller ports we were longing to see. It was particularly hard on those elderly Dutch folk who were whisked to Venice, and thence by train to Holland, just when the catastrophic cold and floods of February 1953 were at their worst. One dowager, over eighty but straight-backed and vigorous, vanished for a day. I asked her friend if she was unwell. "Oh no, she is having her clothes washed. You see she has had pneumonia twice and has to be most careful. She wears the combinations and two pairs of what you call knickerbockers."

In two days we were in Mombasa where we could kit ourselves out. When it comes to buying everything from a toothbrush, clothes and a suitcase to put them in, the insurance money does not go far. I had, still have, my comb and some handkerchiefs, but had been wearing the minimum of underwear and a rather second rate frock and sandals when we ran on the reef, and of course, I had the charity nightgown.

Oddly, whether it was delayed shock I don't know, but in Mombasa I ran a high temperature and found myself in hospital. I didn't feel at all ill, only hot, and it was a bore for Violet, but I enjoyed lying in bed and looking at the blue sea where dhows sailed past into the old Arab harbour.

CHAPTER 18

The Emergency in Kenya

The press had played down the Emergency in Kenya. We had heard that there had been a few murders and a fine old Kikuyu chief had been killed. Just before we arrived some neighbours had been attacked. Like most of us they looked on their staff as part of the family, never locking their doors. Then one night a crowd rushed in and hacked Jack to death, leaving Dorothy for dead. Somehow she crawled to the car and drove into the township. Neither police nor doctor could recognise her. Plastic surgery rebuilt her hands and face and she later returned to the farm, where she ran a health clinic.

No doubt the people of Kenya, especially the Kikuyu, longed for independence, and many took the way of violence. Their weapon is fear. Terrifying oaths bound the taker to the oath administrator. If he or she did not do as they were told, a horrible death awaited them.

All of this broke upon us when we got to Nairobi. It was strange to see European men and women going about armed. Should you put it down for an instant it might disappear, which meant the death of other people. The penalty for loss of a firearm was imprisonment and a large fine. The guilt would be worse.

Before going upcountry we visited Celia's in-laws, as Hugh had been accidentally shot in the knee and was in the military hospital and Celia was in Nairobi. This was our first experience of an old-established coffee shamba, with its stone houses, indoor plumbing and big garden. The coffee, pruned into neat bushes, was laurel green with sweet-scented waxy flowers and bright red cherries. Beyond the regimented rows on the undulating red ground lay the great wave-shaped mountain Ol Donyo Sabuk, and the endless golden plains. This lovely place had been made from scrub-land. Better still, a dry valley now held large ponds of water connected by a fast running stream. The elderly couple found it heartbreaking when their Kikuyu friends would turn away, hanging their heads, when greeted, and that the windows had to be barred and the house locked up at night.

After this we drove up to Thomson's Falls, where Eric and his wife farmed about four miles outside the town. This new farm, called Lokileiti, had 1,000 acres, keeping a herd of pure-bred Friesians. Their farm was just where those red banks used to make travelling so slow in our covered wagon days in the 1920s. Now there was a large brick house built by Italian prisoners-of-war with a good garden. It stood at over 8,000 feet above sea level, bang on the Equator.

The Falls was a thriving town with a hotel, churches, schools, a golf course and a large Co-operative Dairy and the railway, all of which had sprung up in the last thirty years. Fifteen miles on down the old rough

Eric and Joanna's farm called Lokileiti
near Thomson's Falls in the 1950s.

track, we found Eric's first farm near Rumuruti was very much the same, although now there was a bore-hole and dam at the back, so the land could be grazed and the Morogo ran with water all through the year. The little lake the dam made was miles from any building except for the one hut where an old Nandi lived to mind the bore-hole. It was a wonderful place for birds – hammerkops, lily trotters – and I know not what else. Being still counted as dry country the cattle were ranched and Eric had bred back into the hardy Boran strain.

Back up at Eric's new home at Lokileiti, it was much cooler. Two sides we were enclosed by thick cedar forest. Westward lay the river and the falls and to the south was Lake Olbolosat, unseen in the wheat-coloured wide valley with the great massif of the Aberdares on its eastern side. Now there were farms and young plantations as wind-breaks where before there had been nothing but grass. In fact, we could see our neighbours whose house was four miles away, and at night hear their pack of Alsatians answering to our six, which we hoped would act as guard dogs. The barking was maddening but you soon learnt angry barking from conversational and a particularly silly bark for monkeys.

The home was very attractive. Eric's wife Joanna had pieces of old furniture and there were bits from Barton to welcome us. A huge fireplace in the living room was necessary, though when the time came at nightfall for the house to be locked up our servant would make such a blaze of large logs that when it came to cooking supper one wished for the spoon reserved for dining with the devil. Now also one had to remember not to walk between the light and the window.

Violet was given a small automatic, but the only weapon for me was the twelve-bore shotgun. It was a cumbersome thing to hang on to it all the time – going to the bathroom with sponge bag, nightdress, towel, hurricane lamp and gun, for instance. Later I took on making bread for the household, so it leant against the kitchen table just beside me. Still, I did wonder how I'd manage if an attack came when I had sticky dough up to my elbows.

For each of us it was a personal matter whether we stayed and whether we carried a weapon for self-defence.

Progress 1953
Thank God for plumbing!

Thank God for indoor plumbing.

Violet and I made a short trip to Kampala, retracing the route I had taken in the 1920s. Now both Entebbe and the capital were big places. The thatched houses had gone and there was a building explosion. Many-storied blocks were going up everywhere. It was alarming to see them encased in scaffolding of slender branches and bits of bamboo, the builders swarming up and down them like ants.

On our way back we stayed with friends at Sotik, a tea growing area not far from Lake Victoria. Agnes had been left when war started with two small children and a farm just about to go bankrupt. She went to her bank manager and told him that, as a soldier's wife, she was not going to be sold up. He promised to hold his hand, murmuring that pyrethrum was in great demand. So she buckled to. It meant getting up at half past four each day, coping with their herd of cattle, starting a pyrethrum shamba and the bit of tea they had already got in, and somehow educating the children, always reserving a time in the evenings for reading or music. When her husband Brian returned from the war, the place was flourishing. She handed it back to him. Then knowing she must not meddle, but wanting some occupation, she stood as a member for the Legislative Council (LegCo). Her constituency was about the size of Wales with some 300 white farmers living there. Somehow she managed to meet them all and was elected. She was also good friends with the two chiefs of the tribes next to the farm, and would consult with them and hear their views. At six o'clock in the morning she would set off on her 200 mile journey to meetings in Nairobi, driving over rough, twisty roads, a long cotton housecoat enveloping her city clothes, and her dispatch box and gun beside her.

It was bliss to be away from the Emergency-stricken areas, and when we got back to the farm in the Falls, we decided Violet should fly back to England with Joanna. She was feeling the strain, and wished to see her mother who was now well into her eighties. She and Vi went off, and Eric got a friend to give him a hand with the farms and I stayed on to keep house. It was a relief to carry the automatic. Really, we should have handed the shotgun to the police, but we kept the butt up a chimney, the lock piece inside a large Chinese vase and the barrel buried amongst the clubs in the golf bag and got away with it.

One of my jobs from time to time, was to take the cream into the Co-op Dairy. Remembering Kipling's story where the young soldier acted on the old Boer rule that you never come back the way you went, I used to alternate the various ways to the main road, and I would put up a short but vigorous prayer!

Gallant things were happening as well as horrible ones. When a band of men, dressed in police uniform, drove up to a farm, they killed all the household staff but one, who slipped out of a back window and ran to the milking sheds to warn the woman manager who was there at work. The woman manager collected all the women there, armed them with pangas, and led a screaming charge on the house, blowing a hunting horn, which she always carried. The invaders fled.

By now there was civil war in Kikuyu country. The most effective resistance was put up by the Home Guard, Kikuyu men led by young white Kenyan men, many just recently out of school. Bishop

Beecher told me he knew of more than 2,000 Kikuyu who had died for their faith, often tortured for not denying Christ to take the oath. He had taken a Confirmation service to which many of the candidates travelled through miles of dangerous forest. During the service they could see another church going up in flames. Those people knew what they were taking on when they made their promises, but their faith was strong and they were unafraid and at peace.

There were times when I was not. At 8,000 feet the car could come to a stop, the petrol in the carburetor having evaporated. Then Eric would have to syphon it from the tank, whilst I held the rifle and tried to look four ways at once. It was not easy in thick forest.

It was shocking one day to meet a tough elderly farmer in tears. He had built up a beautiful herd of cattle and found them that morning disemboweled and with their legs cut off, and had to shoot the poor things.

One day three armoured cars drove up to the back of the house with a great rattle. In command was a chap reveling in his job, so mustached and slung about with maps, glasses, compass and guns was he. "Just showing the Flag, y'know – it helps morale," he said, saluting smartly. The he asked cautiously, "Is Sheba about?" Sheba, our Alsatian bitch, was there sure enough and the military watched her from the safety of their vehicles, whilst she tip-toed along the line, just longing for one of those warriors to set foot to ground. Even when you knew Sheba well and greeted her politely, she would walk past you in a rather blasé way, and then give you a shrewd nip on the backside.

By this time Joanna was due to return; she came back a very different person, rested and recovered. She had met up with people who asked her why we were farming in Africa, and what we wished to come out of it, which gave her to think.

Later I was picked up by a farm lorry and driven the thirty miles out to where Hugh – still a bit lame – and Celia were living in the manager's house on a big wheat-growing farm. Hugh would put on his uniform and take his chaps on a round of neighbouring huts, looking for strangers and arms. He found the latter as well as a paperback copy of *The Jungle is Neutral*, F Spencer Chapman's book about conducting guerilla warfare against the Japanese in Malaysia during World War II.

One morning a letter came to say that Lokileiti had been attacked and the Mau Mau had been beaten off. Eric had on the farm one lad who had some disease our doctor could not diagnose, possibly some form of parasite causing anemia. The doctor suggested we send him back to his tribal area, but Eric could not do this, for he said the poor chap would only starve. For most of the time he lay by the fire living on milk and bananas, but if he felt better he would potter about. On the Monday when Eric and Joanna went to the milking sheds they found the men silent and unhappy looking, instead of their usual singing and whistling selves. The invalid boy whispered to Eric that the Mau Mau had been there that night and would come to administer the oath on Wednesday.

Eric drove into the Falls where troops were stationed and asked for some men to ambush them. The British soldiers arrived with a great deal of noise, probably thinking Eric was only an old buffer who had the wind up over nothing. Eric hid them in a hut, which would give them a good line of fire, but they fell asleep. Eric's headman had to creep up to the house in the early hours of the morning to tap on the window and whisper that the Mau Mau had come. Eric hurried the quarter mile back to the huts to wake the soldiers up. They opened fire, but to Eric's grief one of his farm hands was mistakenly shot and killed. The Mau Mau fled and next day were nearly all caught. Some had hidden in the swamp, lying under water and breathing through a reed.

After it was all over the headman, who had saved the farm and was a good Catholic, said, "It was good they were driven off, Bwana; for we should have had to drink their oath or be killed. We think you are good people and we like you, but if we had drunk the oath, we would have been compelled to kill you."

A few months later this headman was killed when visiting his home in the Meru district. Maybe word had gotten round that he had saved Eric and Joanna.

CHAPTER 29

To Call the Green Leaf Grey

A short time after this I flew back to England, arriving in the autumn. Sally and Jim had at last got a Council house, so I let mine to an army couple.

It is a most humiliating thing to have the services make an inventory of your possessions. I had thought them rather good, but every scratch or crack was put down with such thoroughness that the list read as if it was so much junk and ready for the next jumble sale. I felt very much for the young couple. He had been a prisoner of war and still suffered mentally from his imprisonment. The most obvious and odd effect was that they piled all the furniture they could into a kind of stockade round the fireplaces. This I suppose gave them a feeling of security, and took away the un-accustomed, frightening atmosphere of an ordinary sized room.

Then I joined Cicely who was in Cambridge, staying with a very dear friend. We found a pokey flat at the top of a Victorian house in the Hills Road, where we spent the winter. Susan was at St Thomas' Hospital and Matt with an engineering firm in Peterborough, so we could see them at weekends and entertain their friends who happened to be up at the University. When summer came we set out in a small car I had bought and visited friends, along with a jaunt round Scotland, in such heavy rain that we got no further north than Inverness.

Back in Cambridge, Cicely's friend offered us her house for the winter, an offer we gladly accepted, for we had fallen in love with the place. We decided to join forces and look for a suitable house. It was a shock to find prices in a university city far higher than in the north, but we came to the conclusion that the important thing was to find the right house, even if we had to dig deeper into our pockets. On a most dismal snowy day in January we found the perfect house standing in what was then a quiet leafy road. It had the right number of rooms with windows looking south down a delightful garden. There was a small garden house where Mary, who had returned from South Africa to join us, said she could practise without driving people mad, and a larger playroom or studio, ideal for parties, film shows and even the building of a cabin cruiser, which a friend achieved, getting it out with three inches to spare.

So, in the spring of 1955, we moved in and lived there for twenty years.

It was a rich life with the interests of a university city, and friends from all over the world visiting us. Cicely's two daughters married and so grandchildren made it even more a real home. We had many joys and some great sorrows to face there.

Cicely was far from well. In fact it was most irritating that a young doctor said, "I can't think why your sister is alive," which he did for six years. Still, however knocked out she was, she would cock an eye and say, "I'm all right."

Susan married and was living in our beloved Kenya and we both visited her and saw that glorious country develop and thrive in a way we hardly dared hope it would.

At last we found the house and its stairs were too much for us. After seeing flats, which seemed built on extremely noisy cross roads and far from any shop or post office – and when you are over seventy the position of the post office matters – we found the ideal spot. Built in a quiet road and looking across the University Cricket Ground, and on the ground floor, it could not be bettered; moreover, it was handy for shops and for our friends to pop in.

There was another great sorting out to be done. Furniture and china could go to members of the family and friends, and as Cicely said on making an inventory, "Isn't it nice to own so few things."

She was running down fast, feeling very weary and bothered with failing eyesight, but she spent a happy year there. Then Susan came over to nurse her. She told me that should she hang on for a long time I would find it trying, so I must snatch a holiday while I could. This I did, seeing her in bed no longer looking like a grey old lady, but gay and pretty. A week later the message came that she had slipped away. She had had our Vicar in, saying that she was dying and wanted a really cheerful funeral. "For the sake of the grandchildren." So they chose joyful and triumphant hymns together.

Now I am on my own, but not so alone, for friends abound, and I escape the bitter winters in the sun of East Africa.

In my late seventies it seems that one sits on the bank of the river of life, not doing so much as being. The banks of a river have been made of so much washed down through the years, and without them the place would be a swamp. Also, one learns more and more that the Eternal Things start here and go on forever. Indeed, every moment we can accept new life if we are willing to accept change around us and within us. We all need this change, this growth, and I pray that it comes to each one of us and to this bewildered world. It's no use waiting for somebody else to start, so one starts oneself. It is a good infection.

I feel truly sorry that with so many blessings I have been given, I have not achieved more. A nature which is tempted to say, "Oh, no," rather than "Oh, yes," is a clog. I am still in some ways the fat child trailing behind saying, "Wait for me," and I cannot put the blame entirely on being lacking in thyroid, or prone to bouts of depression, and the conviction I am a chump. The Holy Spirit can come in and stop the stagnation if one is willing.

There are two lines by GK Chesterton which I treasure:

"There is one sin: To call the green leaf grey,
Whereat the sun in heaven shuddereth."

There are green leaves and lovely valiant lives, and they are the things to treasure, glory in and stand by. The Kingdom of Heaven is truly at hand for us to reach out and grasp. We can listen to the Voice of Wisdom if we will. It's costly but the only commitment that is worthwhile.

So looking at the comic, beautiful and dreadful things that have happened in 78 years, I hang on to the saying: "Behold I make all things new."

That is creating love. Creating is a lovely gift, fresh and new. The world longs for it. May it come to all people. The fresh springs of Love.